Editor-in-Chief: Barrie Pitt
Editor: David Mason
Art Director: Sarah Kingham
Picture Editor: Robert Hunt
Designer: David A Evans
Cover: Denis Piper
Special Drawings: John Batchelor
Photographic Research: John Moore
Cartographer: Richard Natkiel

First Printing: June   1971
Printed in United States of America

Ballantine Books Inc.
101 Fifth Avenue New York NY 10003

An Intext Publisher

Contents

Charles
Buckhahu

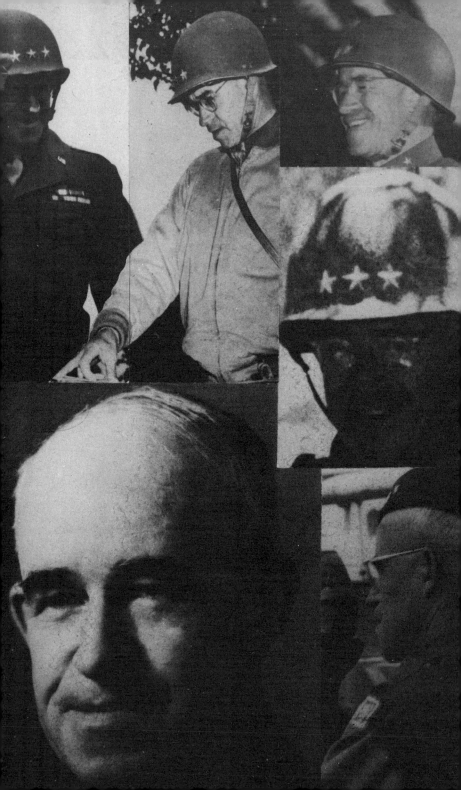

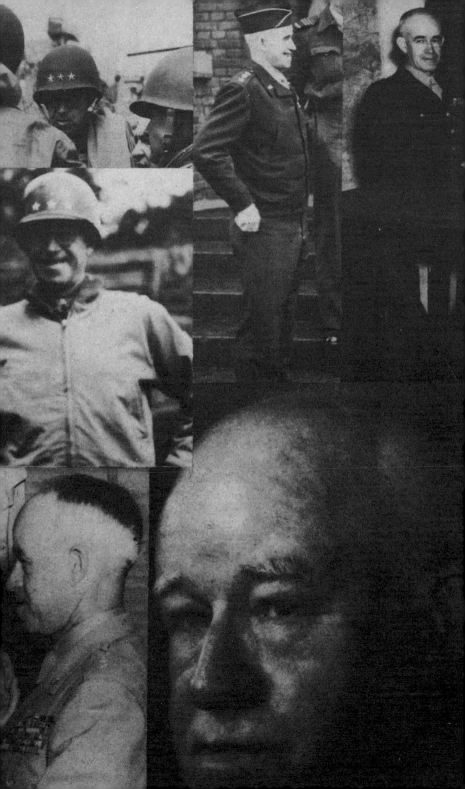

The GI's General

Introduction by Constantine FitzGibbon

From December of 1942 until early in 1944 I was on the intelligence staff of ETOUSA (European Theater of Operations United States Army) and from the late summer of 1943 was, as a very junior officer, marginally involved in the plans for the Normandy invasion (Neptune) and for the larger operation to follow a successful landing (Overlord). When the United States 12th Army Group was created in, I think, early 1944, I was promoted in function. Those of us selected as the embryonic staff of this near headquarters and already in London were moved from Grosvenor to Bryanston Square, and I was put in charge of the German order of battle map. It was my duty to tell our general what our most secret sources of intelligence believed German troop dispositions to be at any time, and therefore what deductions could be drawn as to the enemy's intentions. Since our headquarters was not to become operational until well after we should have landed in Normandy, Bryanston Square was essentially training, as was a trip I was sent on to Algiers and Caserta that spring. At the least a part of that

training was to teach the young man I then was, and the other raw staff officers, the nature of the relationship between the supposed expert on the facts and the commander who must base his decision on those facts as presented to him by his staff.

But our army group had at first no commander. The nameplate of General George Catlett Marshall was, briefly, on his enormous, untenanted office. It was replaced by that of General Omar Bradley, a soldier and a man for whom I had, have, and shall always retain, a feeling of total and quite unabashed hero-worship, an emotion to which I may say I was no more susceptible then than I am now.

In London I saw him almost every day, often more than once. Our relationship was entirely impersonal. I doubt if I ever so much as lit a cigarette in his presence. The only conversation that I recall with him which was not directly connected with his own activities as a commanding general took place in France. He walked into the intelligence caravan one hot afternoon and found me, in a quiet moment, reading *War and Peace*, a book he obviously knew very well. I asked, impertinently, whether he did not see some resemblance between his own position, at the height of a great campaign, with that of Marshal Kutuzev, caught between remote political masters who did not always understand and subordinate generals sometimes impetuous and difficult to control. (And at headquarters at that time we all tended to regard Eisenhower as a politician rather than a soldier.) He told me sternly that he saw no resemblance and since my maps had nothing new to reveal at that hour, he left me to my novel. He himself no doubt returned to planning how best to defeat the German armed forces facing the armies that he commanded: these he never spoke of, and almost certainly never thought of, as "his" armies.

Being a very good general indeed, General Bradley would do much of his planning in front of the intelligence map. There was a formal briefing each evening which he attended accompanied by his senior staff officers. I would then brief him about the day's activities of the German army; Charlie Kindelberger, now a famous economist, about the German air force; another officer on German logistics; and occasionally other experts would follow, such as a ballistics man on the qualities of a new German tank gun, a demolitions expert, and so on. After this General Bradley and his senior staff officers would usually discuss future plans and operations. This was of the greatest value to us junior intelligence officers, since it taught us to see which aspects of enemy activity we must attach particular importance to, amidst the mass of information that passed across our desks.

Nor was that General Bradley's sole daily visit to the I-caravan, or map-room when later we were in billets. He would quite frequently simply drop in, and when other generals were visiting his headquarters, corps and army commanders—occasionally Field-Marshal Montgomery, very rarely General Eisenhower—he would bring them to our map, there to discuss plans and sometimes even to give orders. That was how I came to know General George Patton, and I shall tell one anecdote that illustrates the difference between Patton, the subject of Charles Whiting's earlier book in this series, —I always thought a most unpleasant man—and Bradley himself.

It was September 1944, and by then Patton was in eastern France, closing on the German frontier. We received intelligence of an attack about to come in on his ill-guarded right flank by a couple of German panzer brigades. 12th Army Group was on the move and so, as usual, was Third Army. Our only means of communication was radio, and this item of intelligence was from a source that we were strictly forbidden ever to send over the air. The German attack was to come in at dawn. It was once again mid-afternoon, and I was alone and in charge, for my colonel (Bill Jackson, later President Eisenhower's Special Adviser on Defence) was out; the G-2, General Sibert, was also out and so was General Bradley. There was nobody else whose advice I was permitted to ask as to what I should do. I decided that there were many excellent precedents for disobedience in times of military or naval crisis, wrapped up the information as best I could to safeguard the source, and sent it over the air. Patton moved some armour to protect his flank, and when the attack came in at dawn quite easily beat it off.

Three weeks later General Bradley sent for me, looking unusually stern. 'Read this,' he said.

It was a communication from Third Army G-2 stating that General Patton requested that I be court-martialled for a gross breach of security in having sent that signal over the air. Bradley asked me to explain. I told him what had happened and he said:

'Look, someone's got to answer this thing. I'm a very busy man. Draft a reply for my signature, will you?'

'Yes indeed.' My hero!

Bradley the man

History records that the long-jawed, bespectacled general ate an early breakfast, lingered a little over his second cup of coffee in the swaying wardroom and then went on deck just after five. To left and right the vast armada of thousands of big and little ships still lay silent. The coast that June morning was not yet visible. Weather had forecast there would be coastal mist anyway.

At 0530 hours, the eight-inch turrets of the cruiser, the *USS Augusta*, began to swing slowly towards the shore. The general took the piece of cottonwool proferred by an aide, tore it in two, and stuffed both his ears full. The shooting was about to start. It did, at 0550 hours precisely, when the American vessel opened fire with a roar. The general swung his binoculars round, as the first salvo hushed over the waiting armada. Little violent stars of light erupted along the shore, striking targets which had been painstakingly selected from thousands and thousands of aerial photographs

during the years that this operation had been in planning. The invasion of Europe had begun.

On that sixth day of June, 1944, the general with the homely features sweated out an operation, the success of which could mean the kind of fame which he would not have even dared dream about six months before; but failure would mean the abrupt end to the meteoric career of these last twenty-six months.

At 0645, word reached him that the first wave of invading troops had scrambled ashore. He choked down a cup of scalding hot coffee, worrying now that although the enemy knew the Americans were there, he had not yet opened up with his coastal defences. Two hours later there was still no news from V Corps confirming the landing; the only reports from the shore that the general could pick up over the navy set were alarming and

Lieutenant-General Omar Nelson Bradley

fragmentary. They spoke of sinkings, swamped boats, huddled, frightened men in the sand, chaos and confusion on the beaches.

It was nearly 1000 hours before the general heard from his V Corps commander that his corps had landed, and the latter's message was in no way reassuring. It reported 'Obstacles mined, progress slow . . . DD tanks for Fox Green swamped . . .' Two hours later V Corps reported that the situation was 'still critical' at all four exits from the landing beach. The troops were still pinned down and in part disorganised.

The general now faced a major crisis. With this initial landing hours behind schedule and only part of the first wave of 34,000 troops and 3,300 vehicles ashore, he could now expect the arrival soon of the second wave, consisting of 25,000 soldiers and 4,400 more vehicles. What was he to do? Should he divert the second wave to the other beach at his disposal? But if he did, wouldn't the move materially affect the success of this landing? If he didn't, however, what was he to do with the second wave – allow them to ride off-shore in their transports and face the ever present danger of aircraft, submarines and E-boats? Impotent, helplessly clinging to the radio for some word of hope, the general waited.

At 1330 hours the deadlock was broken. A message from V Corps freed him from his fears. It was from Gerow, the Corps Commander, and read: 'Troops formerly pinned down on beaches, Easy Red, Easy Green, Fox Red advancing up heights behind beaches'. The assault regiments had broken through the enemy defences and were making their way up the cart tracks that led from the 7,000 yard long beach. Soon those cart tracks were going to be – as the general wrote years later – 'the most heavily trafficked roads in Europe'.

Reassured, the general went back to his supervision of the great operation, leaving this beach – 'Omaha' – to

check how the battle was going at his other landing site – 'Utah' Beach. It was going better than at Omaha, but it had its problems too. He helped his corps commander to solve them the best he could, though he knew in his heart he was really almost powerless to change the course of the battle for the beaches; that depended upon a thin khaki line of wet exhausted soldiers.

Late that night, wet and exhausted himself, but confident now that things were shaping up the way they should, he returned to his floating headquarters on the cruiser, riding in the bucking little wooden PT boat that had transported him between the two beaches. Once the general's frail craft was stopped by a US destroyer which suspected the PT boat might be one of the enemy E-boats which had already attempted to raid the beaches. 'What in hell's the recognition signal?' the PT boat's skipper yelled as he scrambled for his signal lantern. 'Give it to me quick, or we'll have the whole damn navy sweeping us with a broadside'.

Half amused and half concerned, the general turned to his aide and whispered, 'I hope he finds it. This would be a helluva way for a doughboy to end the war – skewered on the end of a five-inch shell in five fathoms of water'. But the skipper found the proper signal and the general's boat passed on its way, only to be stopped once more within hailing distance of his mobile headquarters. An air raid had just begun and the officer of the deck of the USS Augusta yelled to the PT boat skipper to 'lie off'. 'But we've got passengers aboard,' the latter protested. 'Prisoners?' the voice in the darkness called from the Augusta's deck through a megaphone. There was a note of curiosity in it now. These would be the first POWs taken that fateful day. 'Stand by to bring the prisoners aboard.' The PT boat 'stood by'. The cold, wet, tired and hungry general climbed up the rope ladder hanging down the cruiser's side and swung himself stiffly over the iron rail.

The sailors crowded forward to get their first sight of the 'prisoners'. Then they stopped. 'Oh hell,' one of them grunted in disappointment, 'It's only General Bradley . . .'

Three years before the man who was soon to command the largest field army the United States has ever sent overseas, was a humble lieutenant-colonel who could look back over twenty-six years of military experi-ence during which he had never served outside the country of his birth or heard a shot fired in anger. In the same year that the man under whom he served on that June morning, Bernard Law Montgomery, was given command of his first corps, and the man against whom he would soon fight, Erwin Rommel, was already considering that command which would bring him world-wide fame, the Afrika Korps, Omar Bradley was still carrying out the same routine garrison duties that had been a daily and some-what dreary part of his life for the best part of the last three decades. At the age of forty-eight years it must have seemed to Omar Bradley that he had reached the peak of his military career when in February 1941 he was appointed the Commandant of the US Infantry School. The post carried the rank of brigadier-general and thus he became the first man of his West Point Class to obtain the status of general. He could go no further. The United States was at peace, the war was thousands of miles away, a matter of the morning newspaper headlines and the evening radio newscasts, and he could now look forward to coasting gently through the years to come to the day of his retirement – a major-general at the most.

Born in Clark, Missouri on the twelfth day of February 1893, Omar Bradley was named Omar for an editor friend of his parents and Nelson for the local town doctor. Save for one and half years in Hawaii, his parents, John

General Bradley surveys Cherbourg after its capture

Smith Bradley and Sarah Elizabeth, remained in the Clark-Highbee area until young Omar Nelson's father died in 1908. The fifteen-year-old high school student and his mother then moved to Moberly, also in Missouri. Two years later he graduated from high school and faced the question of what to do next in view of the fact that his mother, a seamstress, hadn't the money to support him through college. He found a job working in the locomotive workshops of the Wabash Railroad, hoping that in this way he could save enough in order to go to college. But he was fated never to go to the state university upon which his sights were set.

In the late spring of 1911, the superintendent of the Christian Church to which he belonged asked him why he didn't apply for an appointment to the major officer-training school of the United States Army – West Point. 'But I couldn't afford to go to West Point', the young workingman told the Superintendent, John Crewson. 'If I get to the university, I'll have a hard enough time earning my way'.

'You don't pay to go to West Point, Omar,' the churchman lectured him. 'The Army pays you while you're there'.

Young Bradley suddenly became interested in the career of soldier. But he was reluctant to waste his money on taking the necessary examination for entry which was to be given at St Louis. However, when the railroad for which he worked gave him a free pass for the journey, he went. Three weeks later he was informed that the other candidate for the appointment to West Point from his state had failed the exam; he had got the opening. He was to report to Academy on 1st August 1911. He was in the Army.

As a member of the famous class of 1915 which was to produce so many officers who were to make their mark on the Second World War (including Dwight D Eisenhower), he graduated 44th and was commissioned a second lieutenant of infantry on 12th June.

But unlike so many of his fellow graduates he was not fated to see action, either in Mexico or in the First World War. Like his friend Eisenhower, he was disgusted to hear that he had been given a home command; he had been appointed to a guard company of the 14th Infantry Regiment at the Butte copper mines.

When the war ended without his having gone overseas, Bradley felt that his career was over; surely the battle-experienced officers, such as the much decorated Colonel Patton, who had served in France and had been wounded severely, would make the running? But when in 1924 he finished second after Major Gerow (one day like Patton to be one of his army commanders) in the Advanced Students' Infantry Course, in spite of the competition of battle-trained officers who had been overseas, his self-confidence returned.

Over the next fifteen years his career plodded on steadily, full of the daily minutiae of an infantry officer's life in a peacetime garrison army plagued by lack of money, its highpoints a good

performance report from his commanding officer and the very, very occasional promotion. Only two things stick out as significant in those long inter-war years, the salad days of the United States Army: his friendship with Dwight Eisenhower, progressing steadily forward in the staff; and his meeting with the then Lieutenant-Colonel Marshall. For two years Bradley served under that enigmatic American soldier when the Colonel was the assistant commandant of the Infantry School and he, Bradley, chief of the weapons section. Years later when Marshall was made brigadier-general, Bradley wrote to congratulate him.

The new General Marshall replied in a letter which was brief but prophetic: 'I very much hope we will have an opportunity to serve together again; I can think of nothing more satisfactory to me'.

That particular opportunity came in 1940 when Marshall, now Chief of Staff, ordered Bradley to his office as Assistant Secretary of the General Staff. A year later Marshall trans-

Bradley's command ship off the coast of Normandy

ferred him to Fort Benning as commandant of the infantry school. Pearl Harbor came, and again Marshall ensured that Bradley got a field command, his first division – the 82nd Infantry – which was later to achieve ever-lasting fame in its role as an airborne formation. A few months later he got his second division, the 28th Infantry, also to do exceedingly well in Europe later, though occasionally it was dogged by bad luck. Thus Marshall, that strangely reticent commander who did more than any other American soldier to prepare the United States Army for the conflict in Europe and the Pacific, switched Bradley back and forth, ensuring in the short space of twenty months before he finally went overseas that he gained as much command experience as possible; then Bradley, like Eisenhower, figured largely in Marshall's plans for the future conduct of the war.

Generals had always been inclined

to nepotism ever since the days when officers purchased their commissions, and family connections were always much more important than military ability. But in the Second World War there were two outstanding examples of commanders, who promoted not on seniority or even on ability, but on the basis of personal knowledge of the officer concerned. In the British Army, Field-Marshal Montgomery was outstanding on this score, being interested only in officers who had once formed part of the 'Monty-Brookie' team (Sir Alan Brooke, Chief of the Imperial General Staff) or had once been students of his at the Staff College. In the US Army Marshall, rationalising that the average general officer under his command was over age at the commencement of war, often picked men of much junior standing to take over important posts (Eisenhower is a case in point, being appointed to the post of Supreme Commander in Europe over the heads of 366 generals senior to him). And in virtually every case these junior men were officers who had at one time or other served with or under him. Even the overage Patton, who was fifty-six when he went overseas, owed his command clearly to the fact that he was a known quantity to Marshall who had served with him in the First World War.

Thus it was that as 1942 gave way to 1943 General Marshall groomed his protégé, as he had groomed General Eisenhower, for a senior command overseas, though as yet neither Marshall nor Bradley knew what that command might be. But by the end of the United States' first year of war, Marshall was getting around to the realisation that Bradley might be usefully employed under Eisenhower in Africa.

Visiting Eisenhower in Algiers that winter, he felt the major US field commander in the West was running himself into the ground trying to do too much. He told Eisenhower, who was suffering from flu, that 'In this sprawling theater, with demands on your time and attention all the way from Casablanca to Tunisia, you just can't get to all the places you might like to visit. You ought to have a man to be your eyes and ears. Naturally, he'd have to be a man who has ability and someone you can trust . . .'

Eisenhower replied that the suggestion 'would be fine', if they could find the right man. Putting their heads together the two generals began to discuss possibilities. Casually Marshall mentioned Bradley's name, Eisenhower's reaction was spontaneous and immediate. 'Go no further,' he exclaimed. They had found 'Ike's eyes and ears'.

Omar Bradley landed in Algiers on the afternoon of 24th February, 1943, and although the two old college friends had only seen each other a half a dozen times at Army-Navy football games in the intervening years, Eisenhower immediately showed that he had complete confidence in 'Brad'. Giving the latter only a couple of days to acclimatise himself, he sped him thereafter to the front to report on General Fredendall, whose II Corps had suffered disastrously at the Kasserine Pass, taking a beating in the first major battle of American troops in the West. Bradley pulled no punches and did what was expected of him. Reporting back to Eisenhower and asked what he thought of the command situation, he replied. 'It's pretty bad. I've talked to all the division commanders. To a man they've lost confidence in Fredendall as the corps commander'.

Eisenhower nodded his agreement. 'Thanks Brad,' he said, 'you've confirmed what I thought was wrong. As a matter of fact I've already ordered Patton up from Rabat. He'll report in tomorrow to take command of II Corps'.

Thus General 'Blood and Guts' Patton appeared on the scene and for

Lieutenant-General Patton, Bradley, and Major-General Ridgway

Bradley, off the coast of Sicily during the Allied invasion

better or worse, the fates of the two men, Bradley and Patton, were to be linked for the rest of the war.

Patton, profane, outspoken and energetic as usual, did not tolerate Bradley acting as Eisenhower's 'eyes and ears' around his headquarters for very long. Growling 'I'm not going to have any goddam spies running around my headquarters,' he phoned General Bedell Smith, Eisenhower's Chief of Staff, and told him he wanted Bradley as assistant corps commander. He got his way and later, when Patton left the rejuvenated II Corps to prepare his new command – the Seventh Army – for the invasion of Sicily, it was a foregone conclusion that Bradley would get the corps. He did, and Marshall's plans for the reticent, publicity-shy general began to take shape.

However, luck and not planning played the greater role in Bradley's next step up the ladder, which would give him the plum job in the coming invasion of Europe. After an undistinguished campaign in Sicily, which lasted thirty-six days and added nothing to the laurels of any of the senior commanders concerned, British or American, and achieved little save the clearing of the island and the sowing of the first seeds of enemity between Patton and Bradley and their British opposite number Montgomery, chance took a hand. The news leaked out to the Press that General Patton, the high-handed commander of the Seventh Army, had twice slapped soldiers under his command in hospital. The result was a furore in the United States with public and politicians alike calling for Patton's hide.

Patton, who, previous to the disclosure of the 'face-slapping incident,' was probably Washington's choice for the ground commander in Europe under Eisenhower, lost all hope of that post overnight. For weeks he marked

Above: Troops of Bradley's II Corps, US Seventh Army land on the beaches in Sicily. *Below:* Men of the British Eighth Army wade ashore during the Sicily invasion

time at his Sicilian headquarters while Washington decided what was to be done with him. On the mainland of Italy General Clark's Fifth Army started to push up the boot, leaving Patton still without an assignment. Eisenhower left for England and then the worse blow of all came: he was to lose his Seventh Army and his one-time subordinate was to command the American invasion force.

Although General Marshall in Washington was not yet quite prepared to name an army group commander, Bradley was ordered to leave for England and form an army group 'to keep pace with the British planning', though his primary task was to organise the American First Army for the immediate task of landing in France. Thus the II Corps Commander left Sicily to arrive in London in October 1943, opening his headquarters in Bristol on the twentieth of that month. Nineteen months later, when his headquarters finally reached the Elbe in Central Germany, General Omar Bradley would command four full field armies, comprising ten separate corps and forty-three divisions – 1,300,000 combat troops and the largest body of American soldiers ever to serve under one field commander in almost two centuries of American military history.

On 22nd December 1943 the Supreme Commander, General Eisenhower, received a present – two turkeys from Sicily. They came from the still unemployed General Patton who had sent the Christmas present as a gentle reminder that he was looking for a command in the coming invasion. They served their purpose. Amid preparations for his first Christmas in England, Eisenhower drew up the list of officers he hoped to get as field commanders for 'Overlord'. The next day he sent it to General Marshall in Washington. 'My preference for American Group Commander,' he wrote, 'when more than one American Army is operating in "Overlord" is General Bradley. One of his Army

commanders should probably be Patton'.

In early January 1944 Eisenhower visited Washington to review 'Overlord' with General Marshall and then went straight back to London, arriving on 16th January with the command set-up in his pocket. Having no time to see Bradley and tell him the good news, he revealed it in a press conference next day. Thus it was that General Bradley read about the appointments in his morning copy of the *Daily Express* over breakfast at the Dorchester Hotel. But from the *Express's* garbled version of Eisenhower's statement it was not clear to the bespectacled general whether he would command only the First Army or whether he would get the coveted American Army Group. So he went across to Grosvenor Square to clear up the matter.

'It's the Army Group, Brad, just like Monty,' Eisenhower reassured him.

'How about the armies?' Bradley queried.

'Hodges is to get the First Army,

Brad,' Eisenhower replied. Then he drew a deep breath, 'and Patton the Third'.

Bradley's face fell, but Eisenhower reassured him quickly. 'Don't worry, Brad, Georgie won't object.'

Thus Bradley gained the top field command for the crucial campaign in NW Europe. Luck and chance had played a great role in his career in these last months. He owed his good fortune to the fact that Eisenhower had been a little off-colour when Marshall had visited him in Africa and that when he had mentioned Bradley's name, Eisenhower had remembered his one-time sporting companion of West Point; the happenstance that Patton wouldn't tolerate him as 'Ike's eyes and ears' at II Corps headquarters; the unfortunate circumstance that Patton had slapped a couple of combat exhaustion cases in Sicily and had been written off for the top job, so that of Marshall's protégés such as Hodges, Simpson, or Devers, Bradley was the only possible choice for the senior field commander.

The Allied Supreme Command meets for the first time in London

So it was that, as Bradley's troops began to land on that grey stormy June morning in 1944 and push out from the beaches, General Omar Bradley, their commander, was a completely unknown quantity as a general. The limited action in N Africa and Sicily had revealed little about him. There was no popular handy nickname that gave a clue to his character – no 'Ike', 'Monty', 'Blood and Guts'. No personal idiosyncracy of dress – Monty's berets, Patton's ivory-handled revolvers, Ridgway's grenade and carbine – to reveal anything about him. Not one outstanding personal and military trait that could betray the weaknesses or strengths of this tall, broad-shouldered man who was to command the destinies of so many American fighting men and play such a vital·role in the coming campaign. Omar Nelson Bradley was a military *tabula rasa . . .*

Breakthrough or break-out

The details of that first month in Normandy are too well known to warrant much explanation here. Bradley was still only commander of the First US Army and Montgomery was still doing the strategic thinking for him under the terms of the original overall 'Overlord' plan. In the first two days after its critical situation on the beaches, Bradley's V Corps made remarkable progress, and on the 9th Montgomery was able to order Bradley to exploit southwards to St Lô and Caumont. Bradley acted rapidly and by the 11th, his 1st and 2nd Divisions were fourteen miles south of 'Omaha' and had drawn level with the British. Meanwhile his VII Corps under aggressive General 'Lightning Joe' Collins, Montgomery's favourite corps commander among the Americans, pushed forward till they reached Cherbourg in the third week of June.

The fortifications of the great port were formidable and had been specially strengthened to face up to an attack from the rear, which was not always the case with the 'Atlantic Wall' ports. But although Schleiben, the German commander, armed even his cooks with ancient French rifles and requested paradrops of Iron Crosses in bulk to bolster the morale of the defenders, he could not stop Collins. By 26th June all organised resistance within the port had ceased and Schlieben himself surrendered the following day after US tanks had fired a few rounds against his underground well-protected HQ to satisfy 'his honour as a soldier'.

Thus it was that by the 1st July 1944 Bradley's First Army was well established in Normandy. Cherbourg had been taken, supplies flooded in and men were pouring ashore by the thousand in spite of the lack of a major workable port, and Bradley was now in a position to take the next step. As the General saw it, the First Army, confined in a relatively small lodgment

The invasion of Hitler's Europe; US troops land on Omaha Beach

area, needed both elbow room and the better ground to the south which would enable it to fight the war of movement, the type of warfare for which the completely motorised, highly mobile US Army had been designed. It became, therefore, essential to gain terrain which was more favourable for an offensive. But the question was: how and where?

In the last week Bradley conferred both with his corps commanders and Montgomery on the problem, but after considering several basic possibilities for his breakout, he decided that he would pick a soft spot in the enemy line ('the other fellow's line', as Bradley preferred to call the German). Here he would concentrate and break through, following up with a massed push of his armoured divisions. The spot he chose was straight down the west coast Cotentin road from La Haye du Puits through the moors to Coutances. If he could force the Germans to abandon Coutances, the 'other fellow' would have to withdraw across the rest of the Cotentin neck for fear he might be cut off by a pincer attack from St Lô. Thereafter Bradley's men would be in a position to launch the major offensive which would ensure a complete breakout into the heartland of France.

But General Bradley had not taken into consideration the terrain through which his Army was to advance or, if he had, he had probably anticipated that its difficulty would be off-set by the weakness of the German defence. In fact, he assured Eisenhower that this was the 'soft spot' in Normandy, ideal for the breakout. The ground Bradley had picked for his battle was the *bocage*, an area of marshlands boxed in everywhere by six-foot high, tremendously thick hedgerows which could easily stop a tank and were ideal for defence by a mere handful of determined riflemen.

At 0530 hours on the morning of 3rd July, General Middleton started his VIII Corps down the west road, full of high hopes that this was to be the

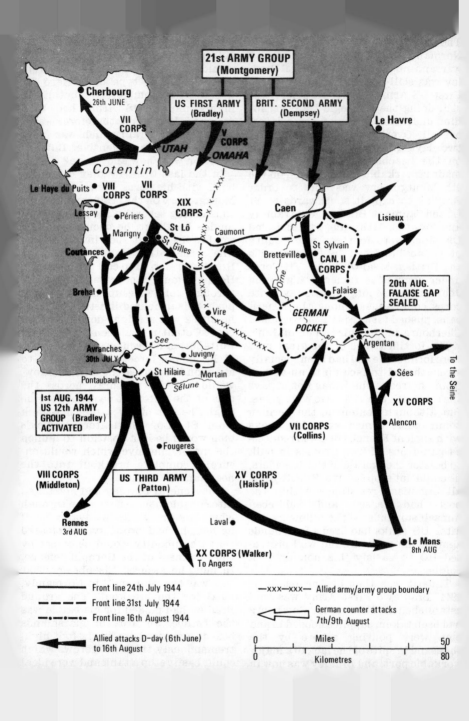

21st ARMY GROUP (Montgomery)

US FIRST ARMY (Bradley)

BRIT. SECOND ARMY (Dempsey)

Cherbourg 26th JUNE

VII CORPS

UTAH

Le Havre

Cotentin

V CORPS *OMAHA*

Le Haye du Puits

VIII CORPS

VII CORPS

XIX CORPS

Caen

Lisieux

Lessay

Périers

St Lô

Caumont

Bretteville

St Sylvain

Marigny

St Gilles

Coutances

Orne

CAN. II CORPS

Brehal

Falaise

20th AUG. FALAISE GAP SEALED

Vire

GERMAN POCKET

Argentan

Avranches 30th JULY

See

Juvigny

To the Seine

Pontaubault

St Hilaire

Mortain

Sélune

Sées

1st AUG. 1944 US 12th ARMY GROUP (Bradley) ACTIVATED

XV CORPS

Alencon

VII CORPS (Collins)

Fougeres

VIII CORPS (Middleton)

US THIRD ARMY (Patton)

XV CORPS (Haislip)

Rennes 3rd AUG

Laval

Le Mans 8th AUG

XX CORPS (Walker) To Angers

——— Front line 24th July 1944	—xxx—xxx— Allied army/army group boundary
– – – Front line 31st July 1944	
–·—·—·— Front line 16th August 1944	German counter attacks 7th/9th August
Allied attacks D-day (6th June) to 16th August	

Miles 0 — 50

Kilometres 0 — 80

start of the big break-out. Six days later he had only advanced a few miles, one 600-yard section took three days to cover. In twelve days of most bitter fighting the Corps advanced eight short miles only. Exhausted and taking heavy casualties the whole time Middleton's infantry battled on. His running mate General Collins with his VII Corps fared little better. Although he continued to fight forward through the murderous terrain in which armor was virtually powerless once it left the roads, he was granted little success and like Middleton he was taking heavy casualties. In the end Bradley ordered Middleton to discontinue the advance on 14th July, still some twelve miles from his objective, the high ground at Coutances. As Bradley was to write after the war: 'It was obvious that the Coutances-St Lô line had become too costly an objective to warrant our insisting upon it as a starting point for the breakout. We would settle, I said, for a less desirable springboard somewhere short of that cross-shoulder line'.

What had gone wrong in this first real battle that Bradley commanded as an army commander? Firstly, there was the nature of the terrain, of course. Surprisingly for an American from a nation renowned for its technical ingenuity, but perhaps understandably for an ex-infantryman ('a doughboy,' as Bradley always liked to call himself), Bradley had not considered any mechanical means of overcoming the *bocage* hedgerow. It was an oversight that had already cost him dearly on the beach at 'Omaha' through his refusal to accept any of Churchill's 'funnies', such as the armoured 'flail' tank, which might have saved him from the many casualties and resultant chaos caused by mines. Secondly, he had underestimated the quality of the German troops opposing him. Again a surprising oversight, for in spite of the fact that these Germans were from a hotchpotch group of formations, most inexperienced commanders tended to over-estimate their opponent in these circumstances. Bradley apparently did not.

But the newly appointed Army Group Commander's third weakness was the most serious. Although he had himself spoken of finding a 'soft spot' in the enemy line and 'concentrating' there, he had done neither of these things. Instead he had attacked along his whole front from the sea to St Lô and since this dispersal of his strength was heightened by the nature of the terrain, he was unable to gain a clear breakthrough anywhere. He had infringed that admirable Prussian military axiom, which had so often brought success to the German army on the offensive – *klotzen nicht kleckern* (group don't disperse). As we will see this was a weakness which was to remain with the general throughout the campaign in NW Europe, not because he was unaware of it but because he was faced with powerful personalities among his generals who demanded their 'share of the cake' in every new offensive.

In the third week of July, Bradley got down to planning a new attempt at breakout and this time luck was on his side. In a way it took the form of two men, one a humble sergeant, the other a general. The sergeant was Curtis G Culin Jr, who in his spare time had welded eight sharp steel teeth to the front of a Sherman tank about two feet above the ground. Equipped with these teeth, which were made from scrap metal to be found in plenty on the battlefield, a tank could drive into a hedgerow at ten to fifteen miles per hour, loosening earth and cutting the roots of the bushes without exposing its soft underbelly to the enemy anti-tank guns, as had been the case up to now when a tank had tried to roll over such an obstacle. Bradley quickly appreciated the value of the invention, awarded the tank sergeant the Legion of Merit and gave out the order that his Army needed a couple of hundred such tanks immediately. Everywhere behind the lines, First Army workshops

The Consolidated B-24 Liberator, with the Boeing B-17, formed the backbone of the United States' strategic bombing efforts in the Second World War, as well as serving in maritime, patrol and transport roles. The type was also used by the RAF. The Liberator was marked by its ability to absorb vast amounts of battle damage and its very long range. Illustrated is the B-24J version. *Engines:* four Pratt & Whitney R-1830 radials, 1,200 hp each at take off. *Armament:* ten .5-inch Browning machine guns with 4,700 rounds of ammunition and up to 12,800 lbs of bombs over short ranges. *Speed:* 290 mph at 25,000 feet. *Ceiling:* 28,000 feet. *Range:* 3,700 miles maximum. *Weight empty/loaded:* 36,500/65,000 lbs. *Span:* 110 feet. *Length:* 67 feet 2 inches

The landings in Normandy presented the Allies with a problem they had not before come across – that of crossing the barriers formed by the *bocage*, the northern French hedgerows. It was impractical to try to scale the banks of earth topped by hedges, for tanks poised on the top presented good targets to the German gunners and were liable to ditch in the effort, so the best solution seemed to be to go through the earth banks which formed the foundations to the hedgerows. The best system for doing this was found by Sergeant Cullin of the United States Army, who invented the 'Rhinoceros', whereby a Sherman tank could be fitted by regimental armourers with two groups of angle-iron cutters on its nose, without impairing its fighting qualities. These would cut into the bank of earth and enable the tank to go straight through rather than over the headgerows. Apart from this modification, the Sherman was unchanged

started to turn out the 'Rhino' in scores.

The general was Patton. On 20th July, with his Third Army still not activated and without a command as yet, he turned up at Bradley's HQ worried over the news he had just received that an attempt had been made to assassinate Hitler. But Bradley wasn't there. Three days later Patton finally contacted his onetime subordinate and, without preliminaries, pleaded with Bradley: 'For God's sake, Brad, you've got to get me into this fight before the war is over. I'm in the doghouse now and I'm apt to die there, unless I pull something spectacular to get me out!' As Bradley was to remark years afterwards: 'I've often wondered, how much this nothing-to-lose attitude prodded Patton in his spectacular race across the face of France. For certainly no other commander could have matched him in reckless haste and boldness'.

Thus armed with a powerful mechanical aid and a bold resourceful cavalry general who thought that this new operation would be his chance to vindicate himself, Bradley continued the planning of his second attempt at breakthrough, which bore the codename 'Cobra'. This time Bradley intended to concentrate his forces on a 6,000-yard front five miles west of St Lô. There, after the completion of a heavy bombing attack, he planned to blast a hole through the German defenses with his infantry and then push his armor and motorised divisions through to the west coast between Coutances and Brehal. In this way he hoped to cut off the enemy LXXXIV Corps, which held the St Lô-Periers-Lessay road. The German commanders, lacking tanks and under orders from Hitler not to yield ground, hoped that they would be able to hold the Americans if they made a strongpoint out of each crossroads, basing their assumptions on the knowledge that the *bocage* would hold up the enemy tanks. They did not yet know of the 'Rhino'.

On the morning of 25th July, th rain clouds disappeared from the skie and weather gave its blessing t Bradley's plan, for he needed clea skies for his preliminary air attack The latter began immediately. Fo two hours and twenty minutes, Foi tresses and Liberators pounded th ground in front of Collins' VII Corps Then at 1100 hours Collins moved foi ward, behind air cover from mediur bombers. Although some of thei bombs fell short and inflicted sever casualties on two units, the attac went in as planned, with the 9t Infantry Division on the right, the 4t in the centre and the 30th on the lef Their objective was the Marigny- S Gilles road, where the two flank divi sions were to swing outwards and thu exploit the gap for the follow-u armour, consisting of the 2nd and 3r Armored Divisions and the 1st Infan try, motorised for the occasion.

With the planes coming in 'as if on conveyor belt' (as General Bayerlein one of the defenders, described the tw day air attack), the infantry reache most of their objectives and the Ger mans started to retreat. Now the wa was open and Collins grasped th opportunity. He flung in his armo and on the morning of 27th July hi 2nd Armored Division was alread thrusting south and south-west fron the Marigny-St Gilles gap. Now th 'Rhinos' came into their own, allowin the First Army to exploit the break through without being limited to th roads as the Germans expected the would be. Whenever a column wa stopped by a defended road crossin or a mined road, the 'Rhinos' swep out of the stalled column and with th aid of bulldozers, cut a by-pass throug the nearest hedgerow. Then th armor would sweep on, leaving th follow-up infantry or engineers to dea with the obstruction.

Back at his TAC HQ, Bradley, wh had been filled with apprehension tha 'Cobra' might fail like his first attemp to break-out, was delighted with th success of the operation which wa

Above: Allied commanders in Normandy; Bradley with Montgomery and Dempsey.
Below: The supreme commander, Eisenhower, with Bradley, Major-General
Gerow and Major-General 'Lightning Joe' Collins

now moving inexorably towards its objective. 'To say . . . that (we are) riding high tonight is putting it mildly,' he wrote to General Eisenhower, 'Things on our front really look good'.

Meanwhile Bradley's second ace, General George Patton, was marking time idly in the midst of this victory. Two days before Bradley had launched 'Cobra', Patton had told his Chief of Staff General Gay: 'I'm afraid Monty doesn't want me because he's afraid I'll steal his show. And Bradley doesn't want the Third Army because he's afraid of Army Group command'. Bradley, for his part, maintained that 'Despite Patton's eagerness to aid us on the "Cobra" attack, for ease of control I was anxious to restrict it to First Army'. And later when Eisenhower urged him to make Patton's Third Army operational and use the dashing cavalryman's skill to assure the complete success of the operation, Bradley balked. 'I assured Ike,' he writes in his memoirs, 'we could more

Above: Sherman 'Rhino' tanks breakout through the bocage. **Right:** Patton and Bradley confer before the drive from Avranches

easily unscramble a jam alone from the First Army CP than we could in conference between two Armies at an Army Group CP'. But on 28th July he finally decided to give Patton some part in the 'Cobra' operation. On that day he told his one-time superior that he would supervise the operations of General Middleton's VIII Corps until his own Third Army became operational on 1st August, 1944.

Patton had a strange concept of 'supervising'. As he soon showed, when he arrived at Middleton's HQ later that same day, he was not content with being in charge, he was going to command! On that particular hot July day, General Middleton, a former First World War infantryman, had only a vague idea of what his Army commander wanted. He knew that he was to continue southwards, but all that Bradley had mentioned he should do in his progress south was to give the enemy 'no time to regroup and reorganize' and '(to) maintain unrelenting pressure on the Germans'. (Several writers on General Bradley have noted his wartime caution in committing far-reaching orders to paper.) Patton changed all that.

The key exit out of the peninsula in which the Allies had found themselves since 6th June had now become the town of Avranches which, lying between the rivers See and Selune, was the hub of a road net converging from north and east. South of the city, the roads merged again, running in a straight line across the Selune to a crossroads, where the roads forked east, west and south. That day studying the map and staring intently at Avranches, a town he remembered from a visit there thirty years before, the 6 feet 2 inch General with the thin pinched face saw more in the town than just a place where he might break-through; he saw it as a site of his own break-out to the glittering prizes that lay beyond.

Thus as the fall of Coutances signalled the end of 'Operation Cobra' – the capture of that town marked the operation's official termination – Patton planned a completely new operation from the one General Bradley had envisaged. As Martin Blumenson, the American military historian, has written: 'Thus ended Operation "Cobra" on the Cotentin west coast in a final action not unlike the last twitch of a lifeless snake . . . Even as "Cobra" was expiring, the battle was passing beyond the limits contemplated for the action. With the Germans reduced to impotence, the offensive was becoming quite different from the original conception'.

Now Patton thrust in his two armoured divisions – the 4th and 6th – bullying and chasing them with all

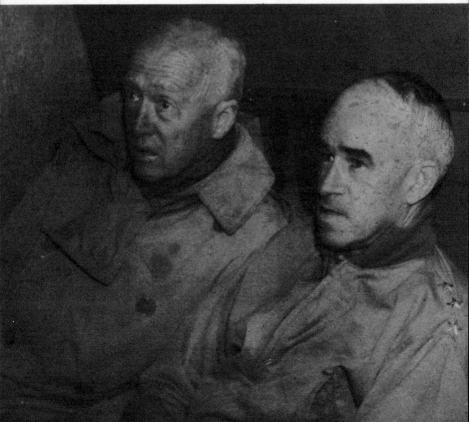

Above: American troops push forward during their advance into Brittany.
Left: Street fighting in the towns on the way to Brest

In this manner Patton whipped VIII Corps through the gap between the German flank and coast. Wood's 4th Armoured Division advanced twenty-five miles in thirty-six hours, reaching Avranches at dusk on 30th July. By the following night it had fanned out on the roads leading from the key town and gained a bridgehead over the River Selune at Pontaubault. The American troops under Patton's command were in Brittany. That same day Kluge, the German commander in the West, reported to Jodl from his Seventh Army HQ: 'As a result of the break-through of the enemy armoured spearheads, the whole western front has been ripped open'. Bradley's Army had broken-*through*. The question of the break-*out* now became paramount, not only for General Bradley, but also for his laurel-seeking subordinate General Patton.

On 1st August, Bradley officially took command of the 12th US Army Group, the American counterpart of Montgomery's 21st Army Group, which presently contained Hodges' First Army and Patton's Third, and which was soon to contain Simpson's Ninth. Patton now became operational as commander of the Third. On that day Bradley ordered Patton to secure the line St Hilaire-Fougeres-Rennes in order to safeguard the Avranches exit while Hodges seized the Vire-Mortain area. Thereafter Patton was then to turn westwards into Brittany proper.

As was to be his wont throughout the rest of the campaign, Patton interpreted his instructions in his own way. He ordered his VIII Corps to drive deep into Brittany immediately. Patton was always prepared to take chances with his flanks and he knew anyway that apart from Ramcke's 2nd Parachute Division, the defenders of Brittany were second-class troops, filled out with foreign 'volunteers' and harassed by the French maquis, which controlled all the secondary roads and several of the main ones.

Pouring seven divisions down the single road that led from Avranches to

possible speed. Once he came upon the divisional commander of the 6th Armored stalled at the 'wrong' side' of the Sienne River, studying a big map with his officers.

'What the hell are you doing, Grow, sitting at the road,' Patton queried in that high-pitched voice of his.

'Taylor is in charge of the advanced guard, General,' the divisional commander replied.

'I don't give a damn who's in charge Have you been down to the river?'

'No, sir. Taylor is trying to find a place to ford it'.

Growling, 'Well, unless you do something, Grow, you'll be out of a job', Patton waded into the river himself to test its depth. Satisfied it wasn't too deep for tanks, he turned to Grow and yelled: 'Okay Grow, take them across. This goddam sewer isn't more than two feet deep!'

Pontaubault in seventy-two hours, with senior officers armed with drawn 45s to ensure order, he flung his divisions across Brittany with a fine disregard for the possibility that an enemy counter-attack on that road might cut off Middleton's whole VIII Corps. But General Bradley was not unaware of that threat, though as yet unaware of the extent to which Patton had 'interpreted' his orders (as Patton told Gaffey, his chief of staff on that first day of August: 'General Bradley simply wants a bridgehead over the Selune River. What I want and intend to get is Brest'. And Brest was two hundred miles away from the point of break-through).

On 2nd August, however, Bradley learned what his fire-eating Third Army Commander was about. Dropping in at Middleton's CP, he found the latter very angry indeed. He had been prepared to execute the operation as Bradley had ordered, but Patton had countermanded those orders. Now he was gravely worried about his exposed

Above: German troops man an anti-tank gun in an attempt to stop the Allies' armoured thrust. *Above right:* US infantrymen move up to take Cherbourg

left flank and rear. 'I'm left with nothing, Brad,' he explained, 'between my extended columns and the main force of the German Seventh Army to my rear'.

Turning the map around, he showed the 12th Army Group Commander what he meant. 'I hate to race on toward Rennes and Brest with so much of the enemy at my rear,' Middleton said. 'If the Germans were to break through here at Avranches to the coast, I'd be cut off way out in Brittany, with as many as 80,000 of my men marooned'. General Bradley's face flushed angrily. 'Dammit,' he said, 'George seems more interested in making headlines with the capture of Brest than in using his head on tactics . . . I don't care if we get Brest tomorrow or ten days later. Once we isolate the Brittany Peninsula we'll get it

anyhow. But we can't take a chance on an open flank. That's why I ordered George to block the peninsula neck'.

That same afternoon General Bradley drove to Patton's CP to take him to task. Patton had just returned from a visit to the front and was covered with dust from the August-dry Breton roads, 'For God's sake, George,' Bradley said, 'what are you going to do about that open flank of Troy Middleton's? I just ordered the 79th (Infantry Division) down there. But I hate to bypass an Army commander on orders to a corps'.

As Bradley described Patton's reaction in his memoirs, 'George smiled sheepishly and put his arm around my shoulder. "Fine, fine, Brad," he said, 'that's just what I would have done. But enough of that – here, let me show you how we're getting on'.

A week later the Third Army was on the Brittany coast and the campaign was over (though Patton didn't win his bet with Montgomery that he would have taken the port of Brest within a week. Brest remained uncaptured till September when it fell at the cost of 10,000 American casualties).

In view of the heavy fighting that broke out that first week in August when the German counter-attack hit the First Army at Mortain, Patton's Brittany campaign, spectacular as it appeared, at least to the pressmen, was of second-rate importance. Montgomery wired Brooke, CIGS, that 'I have turned only one American corps westward into Brittany as I feel that will be enough'. And although we do not have a direct comment on the Patton campaign from Eisenhower, we hear from his intimate, Commander Butcher, that: 'Ike has been impatient, repeat impatient, and I mean impatient. He isn't excited about Patton's armored thrust into the Brittany Peninsula because he figures all that will fall like a ripe apple'. But in any assessment of General Bradley's performance as an army commander, this first 'brush' with his subordinate commander is of

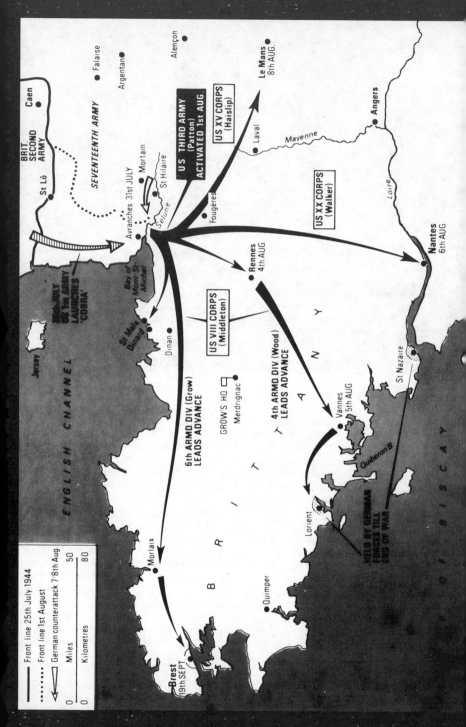

Patton's Third Army seizes the Brittany Peninsula

eal significance. In his memoirs, General Bradley frankly admits he had not wanted Patton in his Group. 'My own feelings on George were mixed,' he wrote after the war. 'He had not been my choice for Army commander and I was still wary of the grace with which he would accept our reversal in roles ... I was apprehensive in having George join my command, for I feared that too much time would probably be spent in curbing his impetuous habits'. And in essence the two men were as different as chalk and cheese. The one: an infantryman, calm and methodical, the product of a poor mid-western home; the other: a cavalryman, impetuous and unmethodical, the product of a rich upper-class home with the tradition of the southern gentlefolk an essential part of the family background. By their very nature these two men had to have a different attitude to war. But in Patton's case this attitude was heightened, some might say twisted by his overweening ambition and desire to repair his reputation which had suffered so much in Sicily. At Third Army headquarters the staff thought that the high command was playing some kind of game with their chief, an attitude that was aided and abetted by Patton's remarks on his superiors. They felt that Eisenhower and Bradley were akin to military parvenus who had little experience of war, but who were eager to get the most mileage possible out of Patton, experienced and always eager to fight. At 12th Army Group HQ, Bradley's staff felt that Patton was somewhat akin to 'Peck's bad boy', ready at the drop of a hat to give way to what Bradley called his 'impetuous habits' and get not only himself but Bradley too into trouble.

In the First World War such a difference of opinion between two high ranking generals would have been solved in the end by the superior of the two getting rid of the other by 'kicking him upstairs' to some kind of training command back home (Even at the beginning of the US entry into the Second World War, Eisenhower had been able to do this with General Fredendall who had failed at the Kasserine Pass, giving him a third star and sending him back to the United States as 'a skilled trainer of men'). But in the Second World War and especially by 1944 this was no longer possible, for a new element had crept into warfare which has plagued harassed generals ever since – the 'communication industry' (press, radio, and now TV). On D-Day there were 530 war correspondents accredited to Supreme HQ and by the end of the war nearly 1,000 of them, sending millions of words 'back home' each day. For the first time in any great war public opinion, especially in the United States, made itself felt on the battlefield. Generals, four or five years before dull 'blimps', were now 'colourful personalities', and soon the generals in question began to believe the correspondents' improvisations, white lies and downright fabrications about their 'vivid exciting' selves.

No other general in the Allied armies held more appeal for the correspondents than tough, swaggering General Patton, with his profanities, his electric personality and highly personal style of going to war. Patton was always good for a story, a dramatic quote, an illuminating insight for the greedy correspondents always searching for new copy to meet the incessant demands of their editors and their public's taste for exciting stories of the war. In comparison Bradley was a colourless personality (in fact Eisenhower remarked that his only weakness was he 'lack(ed) . . . the capacity, possibly the willingness – to dramatize himself') until the 'PR boys' discovered him too and turned him almost overnight into the 'GI's General'.

By the end of July 1944 the correspondents were already creating what were initially artificial rivalries, such as that between Bradley and Montgomery which, according to the cor-

Above: Men of the US Third Army under Patton advance towards Brest. *Below:* US forces advance past Allied tanks during the drive on Brittany. *Right:* The generals discuss the situation; Eisenhower with Bradley and Collins

respondents, was spurring each on to outdo the other. By the end of the Brittany campaign a new rivalry had been created, a much more malicious one – between Patton and his superior Bradley. On the one hand, there was the brilliant aggressive General 'Blood and Guts' Patton, who won the victories – and naturally the headlines too, thanks to his dramatic personality – and, on the other hand, the colourless personality of his one-time subordinate General Bradley, intent on holding Patton back, preventing him as far as he dare from hitting the headlines yet once again. 'Keeping me under the wraps', as Patton himself called it in disgust at the end of the war. (This belief has coloured most of the very partisan biographies written by those close to General Patton. The Third Army commander was a man who inspired intense admiration or dislike. So far only those who admired

Below: **Men of the French** *maquis* **come out into the open.** *Left:* **Crowds of liberated Frenchmen gather to cheer**

'Old Blood and Guts' have written about him).

Thus it was, as the campaign in the West really got into its stride, that the partisan newspaper reports from the various senior headquarters were beginning to create public opinion and it, in its turn, was starting to influence indirectly the battlefield strategy. (Later, if we are to believe some writers, such as ex-war correspondents RW Thompson and Chester Wilmot, it even dictated it).

In the case of Patton, it meant that the 'colourful headline catcher' had always to be accorded special treatment by Bradley who made concessions to his Third Army commander which would have been unthinkable with Hodges of the First Army or later with Simpson of the Ninth. The two latter generals never achieved the same sort of relationship with Bradley that Patton did. And Patton was shrewd enough to recognise this special relationship with his one-time subordinate. Not only did he know that Bradley thought highly of his tactical ability and battlefield audacity, but that the latter gained a kind of reflected glory from his Third Army's exploits. In spite of Patton's apparently naive personality (one of his boldest field commanders once remarked to this writer: 'Patton was ninety per cent psychology and ten per cent fight'. In other words, Patton was not so naive and superficial as it appeared) he knew Bradley needed him and because of this need, he, Patton, could conduct his operations in his own personal and highly individualistic way. Whatever Eisenhower might think of them, there would always be 'Brad' there to protect him from the wrath of the Supreme Commander.

Thus already in August 1944 a special relationship between the two dissimilar generals began to emerge which was going to change the whole character of the campaign in the west and in the end bring about a decisive alteration of the overall strategy of the war in NW Europe.

Enter Montgomery

Shortly after dawn on 7th August Field-Marshal von Kluge, the German commander in the West, launched a massed armoured counter-attack in the direction of the vital town of Avranches. Swiftly it penetrated the US line at the junction between two of Hodges' corps, the XIX and VII. It overran Mortain, the town which later gave its name to the counter-stroke, and rolled on to Juvigny and Le Mesnil-Tove before it was stopped by the 30th Infantry Division, which dug itself in and couldn't be moved, and by Allied air attacks.

Bradley reacted quickly to the threat, having anticipated that it would come anyway. Swiftly he committed General Barton's 4th Infantry Division and the 2nd Armored, which was to become one of his best armoured formations, ranging only after the 4th Armored. Thus when Kluge renewed his attack the following day, using elements of two crack SS divisions, the First Army held firm along the whole line, while General Brooks' 2nd Armored went over to the attack at Mortain. The Germans continued desperately to attempt to break through for another couple of days until, on 12th August, it was clear that the steam had gone out of the enemy counter-attack. That day the Germans started to pull back and Hodges' First Army commenced its drive eastwards again into the heart of France.

The Mortain counter-attack had failed completely; all it had done was to make the German situation in France worse. Now it was up to the Allies to take advantage of the worsening enemy position. Bradley did not hesitate. He called Montgomery, once the threat was overcome at Mortain, and requested his approval 'for a bold course of action designed to encircle the German forces west of Argentan and Falaise'.

There is still some controversy over

who first thought up this encirclement. Montgomery, Eisenhower, Patton and Bradley have all been credited by various writers. Be that as it may, it seems that Montgomery, when called, was thinking along similar lines to Bradley; he readily agreed to the scheme and with Eisenhower's approval, decided to give General Simonds' II Canadian Corps the task of breaking through to Falaise and linking up with Bradley's men coming up from the other side. Bradley, for his part, gave Patton the job of making the link-up.

Simonds attacked on the basis of what Montgomery called 'a wide enveloping movement from the southern American flank up to the Seine about Paris, and at the same time (a) drive the centre and northern sectors of the Allied line straight for the river'. But the Canadians met fierce resistance right from the start. The Canadian 4th Armoured Division overran Bretteville-le-Rabet while the 2nd Polish Armoured seized Cauvicourt and St Sylvain, but at heavy cost. On the 11th and 12th August, the Canadians were still held up on the Falaise road and the town itself was almost twelve miles away. On that same day General Haislip, commanding XV Corps of Patton's Third Army, reached Alençon and Sees, in spite of the fact that Patton was a little suspicious of the heavily-built general's ability to move fast; he considered Haislip was 'musclebound in the fanny' from too much sitting on the well-padded swivel chairs of the War Department in Washington. Swiftly a gap began to form between Haislip and the Canadians.

Montgomery began to urge Crerar, commanding the Canadian Corps involved, to intensify his efforts to capture Falaise, remarking that it was 'vital that it should be done quickly'. ...Obviously,' he told Crerar over the phone, 'if we can close the gap completely, we shall have put the enemy in the most awkward predicament'.

But the German anti-tank defences

were still proving too strong for the Canadian armour. On the 13th they were getting closer to Falaise and Simonds, the Canadian Corps commander, hoping that the Germans would be fooled, ordered his 2nd Division to push to the north-west; he believed that this attack would draw off enemy from the sector of his main effort. But on the evening of the same day a Canadian scout car ran into the German lines by mistake, bringing with it a copy of conference notes which gave away Simonds' whole plan. Thus forewarned the Germans mobilised their last reserves, a dozen odd tanks and 500 SS grenadiers, and stopped the Canadian push on the last ridge before Falaise. There the Germans were still standing firm on the 16th.

Meanwhile General Haislip was in a quandary. There was still an appreciable gap between him and the Canadians. Patton had told him during a visit to his CP: 'Pay no attention to Monty's goddam boundaries. Be prepared to push even beyond Falaise if necessary. I'll give you the word'. Haislip did not think he had sufficient troops to do that. On the 12th, he signalled Patton that now he had Argentan and, therefore, had no further mission.

Patton called Bradley. 'We've got elements in Argentan,' he said, 'Let me go on to Falaise and we'll drive the British back into the sea for another Dunkirk.

'Nothing doing,' Bradley answered. 'You're not to go beyond Argentan. Just stop where you are and build up on that shoulder. Sibert (his chief of intelligence) tells me the German is beginning to pull out. You'd better button up and get ready for him'.

A day later Patton tried again. But Bradley was still worried about the failure of the Canadians to link up and

Left: **Bradley with 'Lightning Joe' Collins.** *Right:* **Montgomery during a visit to his American generals**

the threat of a German break-out of the trap being set for them. General Allen, Bradley's Chief of Staff, answered Patton's plea with 'no'. In spite of the fact that Patton asserted Haislip 'has reconnaissance' beyond the Argentan-Sees line and it was 'perfectly feasible for XV Corps to continue the operation', Bradley had made up his mind.

That day a disappointed Patton told his chief of staff: 'The question why XV Corps halted on the east-west line through Argentan is certain to become of historic importance. I want a stenographic record of this conversation with General Allen included in the History of the Third Army'. Eventually the gap was closed and a fairly large section of the German Army was trapped or slaughtered in the 'Falaise Pocket'. More than had been anticipated escaped; yet the completion of the encirclement signalled the end of effective German power in France, save for the border areas.

It signalled something else: the start of a definite break between, on the one hand, a combination of Patton and Bradley, and, on the other, Field-Marshal Montgomery. Throughout June and July Bradley had loyally obeyed the British overall ground commander, and fully acknowledged his directives. But with the appearance of Patton on the battlefield and his own promotion to 12th Army Group commander, which set him on the same level as Montgomery, who commanded 21st Army Group, a change began to show itself. The Falaise affair was the first sign of what was to come

After halting Patton at Argentan, and thus perhaps aborting a greater slaughter of enemy troops than actually took place, Bradley began to wonder whether he had done the right thing. Should he have halted those five days and let thousands of Germans escape from the Falaise trap? In addition, both he and Patton were infuriated at the slowness of Mont-

gomery's advance and his apparent inability to get the Canadians moving more quickly. Suddenly Bradley began to be critical of Montgomery's ability to command troops and suspicious of his tactics. Scurrilous stories began to course at Patton's headquarters which revealed not only what Patton thought of the British General, but also Bradley. At the beginning of September Patton told a group of newspaper correspondents at his headquarters: 'Yesterday, the Field-Marshal (Montgomery's newly acquired rank was a sardonic tool in Patton's hands thereafter) ordered SHAEF to have Third Army to go on the defensive, stand in place and prepare to guard his right flank. The Field-Marshal then announced that he will, after regrouping, make what he describes as a lightning dagger thrust at the heart of Germany. "They will be off their guard," the Field-Marshal predicts, "and I shall pop out at them – like an angry rabbit"'.

The malicious little tale stemmed obviously from Bradley's statement to Patton a few days earlier: 'He (Montgomery) says he'll make a dagger-thrust at the heart of Germany. But I think it's more likely to be a butter-knife thrust'.

But it was not only the Falaise episode which helped to begin this break about between the two major allied commanders. At the same time as Falaise was coming to a conclusion, the American newspapers were greeting the appointment of General Bradley as overall American ground commander, due to take effect on 1st September. Editors back in the States were asking their correspondents attached to SHAEF for stories about the subject. Meanwhile British editors were asking their men accredited to SHAEF for stories about Montgomery's new position, and whether the Bradley promotion meant an effective demotion for the British general. Fuel was added to the fire, and to the eagerness of the correspondents to get a story on the new command set-up, by

Above: Some of the German Seventh Army escaped, destroying Allied transports.
Below: The killing ground at Falaise; silenced German armour

Above: The Allies destroy bridges on the Seine to cut off the Germans. *Below:* French townspeople cheer as the Allies drive for the Seine. *Right:* US troops take cover in a ditch during the advance across France

the news release that General Eisenhower would come across to France and take up the Supreme Command on 1st September. As a result American correspondents and their British confrères began to take up narrowly nationalistic positions, with the Americans often openly critical of Montgomery and the British on the defensive, trying to vindicate the 'hero of Alamein', seemingly overlooking the fact that the balance of power had changed within the Allied camp; for not only had the command structure changed, but also the ratio

of British to American divisions, with the American formations outgrowing the British rapidly.

Against this kind of background, Montgomery's visit to Bradley's HQ on 17th August, when he proposed that 'After crossing the Seine, 12th and 21st Army Groups should keep together as a solid mass of some forty divisions which would be so strong that it need fear nothing. This force would move north-eastwards' was naturally misconstrued. It and subsequent statements of the same kind that month were interpreted as mean-

US tanks rumble towards Paris

ing that Montgomery was attempting to retain control over all ground forces after 1st September.

It took Montgomery most of that month to realise that the position had changed. Now, instead of being the boss, he was one of several bosses, below Eisenhower and on the same level as Devers and Bradley. But the latter perceived the change quickly enough and also Montgomery's intention after 1st September. In his memoirs, General Bradley writes: 'Monty did not wish to surrender his Army Group command to become Eisenhower's deputy for ground at SHAEF. He would retain 21st Army Group and take on the dual role of Super Ground Force commander as an added function'. Quoting Eisenhower, he goes on to state: '"Monty," Ike said in exasperation,' wants to have his cake and eat it too'".

As a result, with effect from the end of August 1944 General Bradley, ably supported by General Patton, whose dislike of the British Field-Marshal dated back to Africa and Sicily (in

American troops advance on a
farmhouse during the push for Paris

...frica he had felt that his II Corps had
...een dealt a completely inferior role
...Montgomery's Eighth Army and in
...cily he considered that again Mont-
...mery had not given his Seventh
...rmy much more than a flanking role),
...gan to be increasingly concerned.
...irstly with what he considered were
...ontgomery's persistent attempts to
...gain control of all the land armies
...d, secondly, failing this, his attempt
...convince Eisenhower to make the
...ajor push in the north, i.e. in the area
...ntrolled by his own 21st Army
...roup.

...The newspapermen were not slow to
...erceive what was going on. Although
...e mass of them were American,
...ontgomery had some able support-
...rs in such skilled journalists as
...hester Wilmot, Alan Moorehead,
...ifford, Buckley, and Woodward.
...hese latter men enjoyed Montgom-
...ry's confidence and a close friendship
...ith Montgomery's jovial, intelligent
...hief of Staff Major-General Freddie
...e Guingand. They defended their idol
...the best of their ability and two of
...em – Moorehead and Wilmot – con-
...nued to do so after the war in a very
...fective manner. Both groups, Ameri-
...n and British, began to emphasise
...is rivalry between Bradley and
...ontgomery (aided by Patton's dra-
...atic press conferences, which were
...e delight of the Press. As Larry
...ewman, correspondent of the Inter-
...ational News Service, expressed
...atton's effect after one such confer-
...ce: 'That guy in there all by him-
...lf, without the benefit of high priced
...riters, music or scenery, that guy is
...ght-eighty entertainment!')
With the Press feeding stories of the
...valry back to their papers in their
...me countries and exploiting the
...ccesses of their pet generals, public
...inion began to think of the war as
...me kind of race between various
...mies, with the emphasis being on
...e bold deeds of a particular national

group, American, Canadian, British.
(Even within the British forces, a
great deal was made of the difference
between the 'Scotch' and 'English'
divisions, or even between 'home
county' and northern divisions, although such formations contained
soldiers from all over the country and
many a 'Jock' formation was compos-
ed mainly of Welshmen, Irishmen and
naturally Englishmen). Under such
circumstances, General Bradley began
to think more and more in national
terms rather than in Allied ones.

Questions of national prestige, if
not personal prestige, now started to
become paramount, and if we cannot
accept RW Thompson's statement
(and he was a newspaper man accredited to SHAEF at the time) that: 'I
think that it is true that even before
the destruction of the German armies
west of the Seine, not only "logistics"
and Eisenhower's incurable tendency
to compromise, but public opinion,
particularly in the United States,
dictated strategy and saved Germany
from the complete disaster that
seemed about to overwhelm her at the
end of August 1944,' we must acknow-
ledge that from now onwards General
Bradley would not accept any strategy
coming from General Montgomery
which seemed to threaten his own
prestige or that of his armies.

In his memoirs, General Bradley
writes about the Falaise Pocket: 'If
Monty's tactics mystified me, they
dismayed Eisenhower even more'.
But after Falaise Montgomery's tactics were never to mystify Bradley
again. Whatever tactical or strategic
proposals the Britisher was to make
thereafter, they would always be
construed by Bradley, with active
support, as I have already stated, from
General Patton, as an attempt to gain
advantage for himself (Montgomery).
As a result Bradley would fight his
erstwhile ally from here on and in the
end change the whole direction of the
1944-1945 campaign.

September
stalemate

n September 1944 General Bradley ould look back over a month of small nd great successes as an army group ommander. His armies had made , successful break-out from their odgement area, had swept across France to Paris and beyond and in oing so had virtually destroyed (with he aid of Montgomery's 21st Army Group) what was left of the German strength in that country. Now, in that first week of September, his men had completed their sweep through the plains and were, in the case of Patton's Third Army, about to enter upon operations against the enemy troops defending the territory between the Moselle and the Saar rivers. For his part, General Hodges, commander of the First Army, located to the north of Patton, was about to enter Germany itself and it would be only a matter of days before his first armoured columns crossed the frontier into the Reich.

From top to bottom his armies were filled with the heady, contagious feeling that they had broken the back of the German strength in Norman battlefields and that victory was just around the corner. After the Falaise debacle, the men and their commanders asked themselves, where the Germans would get the strength from to defend their frontiers, soon to be breached. Indeed, some of the older US commanders who had fought in the First World War must have felt that final defeat was only a matter of days away when they passed through the Argonne obstacles, where their regiments had bled in 1918, without a fight. On the last day of August Patton's tanks captured Verdun with hardly a blow being struck and hurried on eastwards past those grim brooding heights where hundreds of thousands had died in the old war.

It seemed in September that the overwhelming question was not when but how Germany should be defeated, that is if she were still going to make some pretence at defending her frontiers rather than simply throwing in the towel on the spot? At that time there were four major avenues leading from Northern France into the Reich: through Metz, Saarbrücken to Frankfurt (Patton's front); straight through the Ardennes on a west-east axis (Hodges' front); north of the Ardennes via Maubeuge and Liege (a combined Hodges-Montgomery front); and finally through the plains of Flanders (Montgomery). All these routes could claim some special advantage as the best means of striking across the frontier to the Ruhr (the heart) and then on to Berlin (the head) of the Reich.

According to General Eisenhower's way of thinking that September the best route would be north of the Ardennes in the Montgomery area because firstly the major concentrations of enemy troops were there, and, secondly, an advance in that direction would entail the capture of the port of Antwerp, which Eisenhower regarded

US paratroops prepare to board their transports for Holland

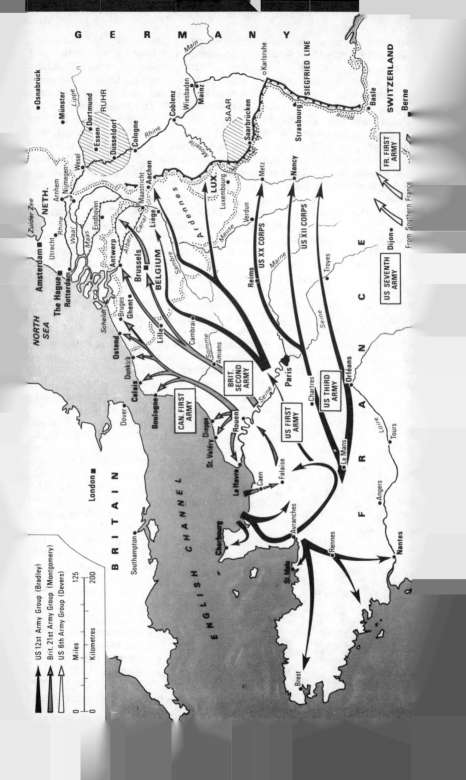

as 'a permanent and adequate base' essential in any operation that took his troops to and over the Rhine. However, in spite the priority he felt should be given to Montgomery, Eisenhower also believed that there should also be subsidiary thrust east via Metz (Patton). On this latter point Montgomery and Eisenhower stood in fundamental disagreement and were going to continue to do so for the rest of the war until the issue solved itself. Montgomery characterised the Eisenhower plan as the 'broad front policy,' and his own as the 'single thrust theory'. For Montgomery the war could only be won rapidly (and because of Britain's manpower position it had to be won rapidly now) by 'one powerful full-blooded thrust across the Rhine and into the heart of Germany, backed by the whole resources of the Allied armies' – 'the forty divisions,' he was always dreaming about. The birdlike little British commander demanded that his front should have the sole priority for men and supplies so that he could force the West Wall and 'bounce' a crossing across the Rhine, to use Montgomery's own typically unfortunate phraseology, while the enemy was still in full retreat. But there was a fly in the ointment: the question of prestige.

It was natural, of course, that Eisenhower's decision to give priority to Montgomery's drive in the north was not welcomed with open arms by Bradley and his subordinate who would be most affected, General Patton. After only one month as Army Group Commander and having finally manged to establish himself as a separate entity, away from Montgomery's control, with the number of American soldiers in Europe rapidly outnumbering the British, Bradley was now suddenly faced with the prospect of playing second fiddle. The prospect was even more bitter in view of the fact that Patton's Third Army had reached a position thirty miles from Metz and seventy from the Saar on the last day of August, with apparently

nothing in its way save the West Wall fortifications, reputedly unmanned at this time.

Thus it was that, although he tried to be objective and in some ways well understood the priority given to the northern attack, he felt that he could not totally accept Eisenhower's ruling. On 4th September, Eisenhower issued a directive, ordering the forces north-west of the Ardennes (ie Montgomery's 21st Army Group and two corps of the US First Army) 'to secure Antwerp, reach the sector of the Rhine covering the Ruhr and then seize the Ruhr'. Allied forces south of the Ardennes (ie Patton's Third Army and one corps of the US First Army) were to 'occupy the sector of the Siegfried Line covering the Saar and then seize Frankfurt'. However in his directive Eisenhower made it quite clear that the northern thrust must have priority. Referring to the Third Army, he pointed out that 'This operation should start as soon as possible, but the troops of the Central Group of armies (Bradley's) operating against the Ruhr north-west of the Ardennes must first be adequately supported!'

But at the crucial period when Eisenhower should have been ensuring that his directive was carried out, he was immobilised in his villa on the French coast at Granville (the villa was named 'Montgomery'). On 2nd September, returning from a flying trip to Bradley's CP for a conference, his little L-5, a liaison plane, had been forced to land on the beach. Helping to push the plane up the beach to higher ground because of the tide, Eisenhower badly twisted his knee. Now he was forced 'to sit with his leg straight' (as Commander Butcher recorded) 'and is quite uncomfortable. But worst of all, the stiff leg makes difficult his normal movement around the country to see the commanders'.

Thus Eisenhower was too far away personally to interfere when Bradley decided that he need not hold Patton back; in spite of the fact that the

Left and above: Montgomery's attempt to 'bounce the Rhine'; C-47 transports and gliders on their way to Arnhem and Nijmegen

northern operation against the Ruhr 'must first be adequately supported,' which would mean 5,000 tons of supplies per day for the First Army and 2,000 for the Third. Two days after Eisenhower suffered his unfortunate accident, Bradley had come to the conclusion that 'the situation in the north having been stabilised', Patton would get 'half of the available supplies and could cross the Moselle and force the Siegried Line'. In addition, Hodges would have to suffer the loss of his V Corps to reinforce the Third Army, switching from the First's centre to cover Patton's northern flank as he drove for the Saar and Germany beyond.

On 17th September, Bradley called Patton in some excitement to tell him that Montgomery wanted to stop the Third because he was ready for the second phase of his drive north. Bradley did little to conceal either his anger or his contempt for his British opposite number. Patton told his boss not to worry. 'In view of Monty's ambitions,' he said over the phone, 'I'll get so involved that they won't be able to stop me. Eddy (one of his corps commanders) will start tomorrow morning for the West Wall and then we'll be off running. So play it dumb, Brad. Don't call me till after dark of the 19th. After that we won't have any reason to worry about Monty's dagger-thrust'.

This was a typical Patton dodge to involve himself in action although he wasn't authorised to do so. First he would order a reconnaissance which, once it got itself involved with the enemy would be progressively built up until Bradley found himself with a minor battle on his hands and could report to Eisenhower that Patton would have to be supported now or suffer a defeat.

At the same time that Bradley gave

The September stalemate: British paratroops in defensive positions

Patton the green light to go ahead on the Moselle, he also ordered the attack on the port of Brest, well to the Allied rear and about which he and Patton had agreed: 'the taking of Brest at the time was useless because it was too far away and the harbor was too badly destroyed'. Yet in spite of the probable uselessness of the port and the importance of the drive north, Bradley ordered on 12th September that 'the armies will have equal priority in supply except that the capture of Brest will have first priority'. So Middleton's 80,000 strong VIII Corps was involved too in operations which not only cost 10,000 casualties for a prestige objective but also consumed valuable fuel and transport at the time when these two items were at a premium.

It is clear, therefore, that by September General Bradley was not prepared to 'adequately support' Montgomery's drive north. He felt that he surely deserved a piece of the cake as the commander of the major component of the Allied armies. However, if he supported Montgomery and Hodges as Eisenhower had presumably envisaged, then his remaining army, the Third, would be virtually immobilised and his own reputation would suffer. Further, in his attempt to keep his own personality before the public, he was aided and abetted by General Patton, a naturally flamboyant personality, who was only too eager to flaunt authority in the form of Eisenhower and Montgomery.

The result was that Montgomery had to rely almost completely on his own resources for Operation Market Garden (his attempt to 'bounce' the Rhine by the paradrops at Nijmegen and Arnhem) while Hodges, whose troops had crossed the German frontier at Prum on the evening of 11th September became so bogged down in the fighting around Aachen a couple of days later that they were unable to aid Montgomery.

By the end of September and the failure of Montgomery's attempt to rush the Rhine at Arnhem, any possibility that the war would be over by Christmas was abandoned. The German Army in the West had regained its balance after the debacle of France and had been able to form a coherent line along the German frontier. Patton was engaged in heavy fighting at Metz and in the Saar and even that incurable optimist no longer believed in a Christmas victory. Further north, Hodges had stalled at the Aachen Gap and was similarly bogged down in heavy fighting, and even the arrival of a new American army – the Ninth under General Simpson – which took its position in the line between Montgomery and Hodges did not change the balance of events. Montgomery had stalled too and his Army was now prepared for the bitter slog through Holland. In spite of Eisenhower's attempts to lay down priorities and avoid the defects of a broad front strategy, the end of September 1944 saw every Allied army, including Devers' Seventh, which had come up from the south, engaged in operations all along the huge front, soon again to be threatened by the problem of 'the life-blood of supply (which) was running previously thin through the forward extremities of the Army,' (as Eisenhower put it).

It was clear that Allied strategy had to be reconsidered and on 18th October, General Eisenhower conferred with Bradley and Montgomery in Brussels to discuss their plans for the winter. There it was decided to make another major effort to reach the Rhine and gain a bridgehead before the onset of winter. Montgomery pointed out forcefully that the success of this new attempt would depend upon Bradley not undertaking any major offensive south of the Ardennes.

The Supreme Commander did not altogether accept Montgomery's objection to any major effort being undertaken by either Patton's Third Army or Devers' Seventh, but he did agree that the major aim was the Ruhr in the north and that an attempt

Major-General Robert W Grow

Lieutenant-General Courtney H Hodges

to reach it should be made with two armies. This time the attempt to reach the Rhine, cross it and penetrate into the Ruhr would be under Bradley's command and not Montgomery's. The American would launch the First and Ninth Armies through the Aachen gap at the beginning of November, with the First aiming for Cologne and Bonn and the Ninth for Krefeld. As for Patton's Third, no date was set for an attack on its part. When logistics permitted it would join in with, as Eisenhower's directive expressly put it, 'a subsidiary' operation 'so timed as best to assist the main effort in the north'.

But Patton, impatient as ever to get into action, convinced Bradley that he was ready to 'jump off on twenty-four hours notice,' in spite of the fact that the weather on his front was terrible, bogging down his armor and supply columns. As a result Bradley gave his subordinate the green light, and the latter sprang into action, assuring one of his divisions to whom he talked before the attack that 'It is 132 miles to the Rhine from here, and if this army will attack with venom and desperate energy, it is more than probable that the war will end before we get to the

Rhine. Therefore, when we attack, go like hell!'

But the rains still poured down on his front; so much so that just prior to his offensive on 7th November, while Patton was praying and reading his Bible, two of his senior commanders burst into his headquarters and began to plead with him to call off the attack. 'The attack will go on,' Patton told them severely, 'rain or no rain. And I'm sure it will succeed.'

When the Corps Commander, Lieutenant-General Manton Eddy, insisted that the jump-off day should be postponed, Patton grew angry and told Eddy and his divisional commander Grow, 'I think you better recommend the men you would like appointed as your successors.'

The offensive began on time. But the weather defeated Patton and his drive bogged down rapidly. By then, however, the negative influence it had wielded upon Hodges and Simpson's major thrust north of the Ardennes was already being felt. Ammunition was generally in short supply due to the overconfident optimism of the armament industry back in the United States, which had begun to slacken off production in the summer of 1944

Montgomery and General Horrocks survey the Albert Canal

when victory had seemed just around the corner. Now supply could not bring up enough ammunition to substain protracted operations on two fronts, especially as Hodges' First Army, involved in the hard slog against the fixed defences of Aachen and its surrounding area, needed large supplies of artillery shells. The ammunition crisis, in fact, became so acute that the Supreme Commander himself was forced to make a special radio broadcast to the United States appealing to the factory workers for increased output. Thus it was that Patton's operations in the Moselle-Saar area consumed vast quantities of ammunition vitally needed that November by Hodges and Simpson further to the north.

So as November 1944 gave way to December, stalemate reigned again along the long front under General Bradley's command. Both his major offensive north of the Ardennes and his minor one to the south of the rugged forest area had come to a stop and deteriorated into sporadic regimental and battalion-sized operations. Now Montgomery once again took up his cudgel against Eisenhower's over-all strategy. This time instead of using his old argument that the reason for Allied failure was Eisenhower's insistence on the broad front strategy instead of his own 'narrow front thrust,' he took a fresh approach. 'The theatre divides itself naturally into two fronts,' he wrote at that time, 'one north of the Ardennes and one south of the Ardennes. We want one commander in full operational control north of the Ardennes and

And it was obvious who he thought the northern commander should be –

– Bernard Law Montgomery.

Eisenhower did not agree, altogether. 'In regard to the division of the command,' he replied to Montgomery's letter, 'We must choose the best line of attack to assure success . . . from my personal viewpoint it would be simpler for me to have the battle zone divided into two general sectors in each of which one individual could achieve close battle coordination. I expressed some doubt whether this zone should be divided on the basis of our rear areas or on the basis of natural lines of advance into Germany. There was some question in my mind whether the Ardennes or the Ruhr should mark the dividing line, if such a plan should be adopted'.

Thus, while it was obvious to any objective observer that General Bradley's Army Group was no longer a cohesive force and that Patton's drive to the Saar had pulled the Group out

of shape, with Hodges' and Simpson's operations having a much closer relationship to Field-Marshal Montgomery's operations in the north than to Patton's or Devers' in the south, nothing was done save talk.

At this particular period of the war, national and personal prestige began to emerge as the decisive factor. They were more important than that of the correct strategy which would win the war quickly and economically.(And in writing this, I am not forgetting that Montgomery's claims for the full weight of Allied pressure to be brought to bear in his sector were also motivated, to a certain extent, by his own desire for personal and national recognition. Though in his defence, one must point out that he twice offered to allow General Bradley take over overall command of the ground forces if this meant one decisive major stroke would be made).

But now the ball had passed to the enemy's court. While the Allied commanders sat on their fingers and talked and talked, Adolf Hitler and his military advisers had begun to realise the importance of that gigantic hinge to the whole Allied front – the Belgian Ardennes. The thinly held Ardennes – some four American divisions holding a front of some sixty miles in length – was already under active German scrutiny from October onwards as the possible site of the last German counter-offensive of the war in the west: the one which Adolf Hitler hoped would bring about the decisive turning point in his relationships with the Allies. Even if he did not completely win the battle he planned for the area, at least he might postpone the end of the war for several months and obtain better peace terms than the uncompromising one of 'unconditional surrender'. The events and mistakes of October and November were leading inexorably to that surprise German offensive which one day soon was to be called the 'Battle of the Bulge'.

Fiasco
in the
Ardennes

As dusk descended upon northwest Europe on 16th December 1944, General Eisenhower was engaged in conference with General Bradley at his Versailles HQ on the problem of finding sufficient reinforcements to fill the gaps in the infantry divisions which had been badly hit in November. On that particular grey day Montgomery had sent his boss a written request for Christmas leave, adding he'd like to collect the five pound bet he had made with Eisenhower that the war wouldn't be over by Christmas. With a chuckle 'Ike' had remarked he still had nine days to go before he needed to pay. After approving Montgomery's request, Eisenhower had given the bride away at his favourite orderly's wedding, had a couple of glasses of champagne and was now trying to hammer out policy with Bradley as to how they might find more riflemen for the front.

The six soldiers involved were sitting around in Eisenhower's office informally when the deputy chief of intelligence Brigadier-General Betts suddenly made an appearance. He seemed pale and shaken and asked if he might see his boss Major-General Kenneth Strong. The tall British officer followed him to the door and returned a few moments later to announce solemnly, 'Gentlemen, this morning the enemy counterattacked at five separate points across the First Army sector?' General Bedell Smith, Eisenhower's hot-tempered chief-of-staff, was the first to react. Turning to Bradley, he said that the 12th Army Group Commander had been warned of such a possibility, to which Bradley replied (according to General Strong) that 'in anticipation of this event he had two divisions ready to intervene'.

He went on: 'The other fellow knows that he must lighten the pressure Patton has built up against him (he meant Patton's attack in the Saar). If by coming through the Ardennes he can force us to pull Patton's troops out

of the Saar and throw them against his counteroffensive, he'll get what he's after. And that's just a little more time'.

'This is no local attack,' Eisenhower replied to Bradley's attempt to minimise the German offensive. 'It's not logical for the Germans to launch a local attack at our weakest point'.

'If it's not a local attack, what kind of attack is it?' Bradley asked. Eisenhower shrugged. 'Now that remains to be seen. But I don't think we can afford to sit on our hands till we've found out'.

'What do you think we should do then'?

'Send Middleton (General Middleton commanding the US VIII Corps in the Ardennes) some help. About two divisions'.

'I suppose,' Bradley said thoughtfully, 'that would be safer. Of course, you know one of those divisions will have to come from Patton'.

'So?' Eisenhower reacted.

'So – Georgie won't like losing a his division a few days before big attack on the Saar'.

'You tell him,' Eisenhower said angrily, 'that Ike is running this damned war'!

Thus the great counter-offensive which would bring about the greatest personal crisis in Bradley's professional life started. In his memoirs there is no clue to his reactions to Strong's news that December afternoon. All we have is his candid admission of 'how grossly I had underrated the enemy's intentions in thinking the offensive a spoiling attack'. Yet one wonders in retrospect if he took the news so lightly then. As we shall see, General Bradley must accept the responsibility for the weakening of the Ardennes sector and for not anticipating that the enemy might take advantage of his weakness there. But more of that later.

On that evening General Middleton's VIII Corps in the Ardennes had been definitely breached in several areas by three strong German armies, two of

US tank and tank-destroyer prepare to engage the enemy

Field-Marshal Model

But then Bradley was not alone in his underestimation of the enemy's intention although by the end of the first day of the counter-offensive some seventeen major enemy formations had been already identified by General Strong's intelligence men. As Robert Merriam, the Ninth Army historian who was present in the Ardennes, has written: 'Our forces reacted slowly, and only slowly did the news of the forceful German attacks trickle up the chain of command to Paris . . . Although claims have been made that Eisenhower gauged instantly the seriousness of the situation, the truth is that none of the Allied commanders from Eisenhower down, realized the true extent of the German attack on that first day'.

At the end of that thirty-six hour period, Bradley, who had been contented to wait and see what might happen all through the 17th, finally began to become a little alarmed. It was not until the third day of the German attack (18th December) that he ordered Patton to cancel his Third Army offensive planned to start in the Saar on 21st December and to start planning a counter-attack to hit the enemy's southern flank. But by that time some thirty-six German divisions had been identified and the 'bulge', that wedge into the Belgian Ardennes westwards, had already been established. The situation was dangerous, alarm and confusion were wide-spread in the Allied rear areas, and Middleton's front had virtually crumbled, though American troops were holding both shoulders of the German penetration of the US line. It was within those same thirty-six hours that General Bradley made a seemingly relatively minor decision which was going to affect the course of his role in the coming battle considerably. After spending the night of 16/17th December at Eisenhower's headquarters, Bradley and his aide, Colonel Hansen, left Versailles and drove to Bradley's main headquarters in Verdun, where a machine-gun jeep was waiting to

them armored. Although Hitler's own plan for the offensive was an ambitious thrust forward between the British and American armies to the Allies' major supply port, Antwerp, his field commanders were hoping only to reach the River Meuse which in itself would be quite an achievement in Germany's fifth year of war. (Field-Marshal von Rundstedt said he would go down on his knees and pray if that more modest aim was realised). There on the Meuse they could form a strong defensive line and probably put the Allied time-table for the invasion of the Reich back several months – at least, until spring. But both the Hitler plan and that of his field commanders depended upon the speed of the German advance and the slowness of the American reaction.

For the next thirty-six hours General Bradley played into their hands. He accepted Eisenhower's advice to send an armored division to each end of the Ardennes front. He allowed General Hodges to continue his attack on the Roer river area. He failed to go to Middleton's VIII Corps and see for himself the seriousness of the situation which would soon entail one of his divisions being completely surrounded and the other badly cut up.

Field-Marshal von Rundstedt

Major-General Troy Middleton

escort him to his advance HQ at Luxemburg. On the road to the little capital he noted a huge American flag hanging from the roof of a modest stone cottage. Turning to Hansen, he said: 'I hope he doesn't have to take it down'. 'You mean we'll stay put in Luxemburg?' Hansen asked. 'You can bet your life we will,' General Bradley said firmly, 'I'm not going to budge the CP. It would scare everyone else to death'. Then the two men drove on in silence to Bradley's TAC HQ, located in a hotel opposite Luxemburg station where the commander remarked to his chief of staff General 'Lev' Allen: 'Pardon my French, Lev, but just where in hell has this sonuvabitch gotten all his strength'.

Thus Bradley intentionally positioned himself in Luxemburg to the south of the Bulge and far away from the major action in the decisive initial phase of the Battle, for this took place primarily in the north. And there the 12th Army Group commander was to remain for the rest of the Battle while the enemy drove a deep wedge between Hodges' First Army and Patton's Third and in doing so jeopardised his effective control of the whole battle-field: a vitally important issue soon to be raised, and solved in a manner that

was to occasion lasting resentment and more in the person of Omar Bradley.

Then after the first shock occasioned by the German surprise attack had worn off, the American command began to react and General Eisenhower called a conference of his senior officers concerned: Bradley, Devers, Patton, etc, etc. They were to drive to Eagle Main, Bradley's Verdun HQ, where Eisenhower would brief them on the Ardennes and discuss with them the most effective measures to deal with the German threat. The conference would begin on the morning of the 19th of December in the old French Maginot Caserne. The officers who attended the Verdun conference that morning were tense enough as they took their places in the old squad room of the ex-French barracks, which was heated by a sole pot-bellied stove. The British officers, in particular, were worried that the Americans might not have the ability to deal with the new situation, which was beginning to take on alarming dimensions. However, General Eisenhower, though facing a great personal crisis as Washington would expect him to take the responsibility for any failure to anticipate the sudden enemy attack,

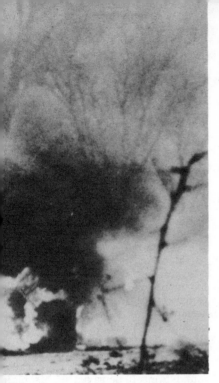

above: German troops advance during the last offensive on the Western Front
left: Captured American equipment during the German advance on Bastogne

id not appear to share the general enseness. Looking around the assembled officers, he announced: 'The resent situation is to be regarded as ne of opportunity for us, and not one f disaster'. He paused and smiled. There will be only cheerful faces at his conference table'.

Patton reacted immediately: 'Hell, t's have the guts to let the sons of itches go all the way to Paris,' he norted. 'Then we'll really cut 'em off nd show 'em up'!

After that the ice was really broken nd the conference got down to business. General Strong briefed the members on the intelligence situation efore Eisenhower took over and xplained his plan was based primarily n a 'counterattack on the southern ank' (of the German penetration). He urned then to Patton and snapped,

'George, I want you to go to Luxemburg and take charge of the battle making a strong counterattack with at least six divisions'.

Patton accepted the order without turning a hair, although it meant extricating his divisions from the front line in the Saar, swinging them around at a ninety degree angle and – in terms of logistics – moving 133,178 motor vehicles over 1.6 million road miles in the depth of winter. In fact, he told Eisenhower he would be able to attack with three of his divisions two days earlier than the Supreme Commander thought possible.

Thereafter the conference broke up into study groups, with both Patton and then a little later Bradley returning to Luxemburg post-haste to carry out the new plan. As we have seen the plan was simple enough; it was to be a flank attack carried out to the south by Patton's Third Army, who would come directly under Bradley's command for the battle, then both their forward headquarters were going to be located in the same town – Luxemburg. There had been no mention of an alternative plan or an alternative commander. Thus it seemed that the Verdun conference had decided completely the American reaction to the German threat. Yet within twelve hours of the Verdun conference, far-reaching, completely new decisions, not even touched upon at Verdun, were being made.

What happened in the next twelve hours is not yet clear, even after a quarter of a century in which most of the major participants in the events of those hours have tried to explain their actions on paper; and it is doubtful that we will have a truthful explanation of what really happened until the last of the participants has died. As it stands now, we know that when General Strong, Eisenhower's chief of intelligence, returned to Versailles, he found the situation at the front had deteriorated dramatically. The points of the German breakthrough had been extended significantly and more and more first class German formations were being identified by the hour. Fearing that the Verdun measures were not sufficient and might even be too late he contacted Major-General John Whiteley, Eisenhower's Assistant Chief of Staff. Like himself General Whiteley was a British officer and, it must be pointed out, extremely loyal to Eisenhower, pro-American and no great admirer of Field-Marshal Montgomery. Yet on that evening the two British officers decided to approach Whiteley's chief General Bedell Smith with a proposal which both men knew full well would cause a sensation – Montgomery should take over the northern flank of the Bulge!

This would mean that a large number of American troops, in particular, Hodges' First Army, would come under the command of a British commander, although at present no British troops were participating in what was a completely American battle. In addition, it would mean a considerable revision of the Verdun decisions taken that morning, which would not be accepted gracefully by either the American generals, who mostly disliked the British Field-Marshal, or the American public, who would not understand why a Britisher should command so many American soldiers. But most importantly, it meant that the reputation of America's major field commander, General Bradley, already damaged by his inability to foresee the German counter-attack, would be grossly slurred. Bradley, the American public might decide, was obviously not fit to command US troops in an emergency; the job had to be given to a foreigner.

It was to be expected that when the two British officers presented their suggestion to Bedell Smith around midnight that the hot-tempered American officer told them (as General Strong described it much later) that 'because of the view we had taken of the situation neither Whiteley nor I could any longer be acceptable as staff officers to General Eisenhower. Ne[xt] day instructions would be issue[d] relieving us of our appointments a[nd] returning us to the United Kingdo[m] This looked like a sad ending.'

Next morning, however, when t[he] two British officers turned up for t[he] usual briefing, the situation ha[d] changed drastically. Bedell Smith to[ld] them to keep their mouths shut abo[ut] what had happened the night befor[e] he would make their suggestion [to] Eisenhower himself. As General Stron[g] describes the scene: 'Eisenhow[er] listened without speaking to wh[at] Bedell Smith said; then he picked u[p] the telephone and asked to be p[ut] through to General Bradley. A lon[g] conversation ensued of which w[e] naturally could hear only one end, b[ut] General Bradley was obviously pr[o]testing strongly, for the conversatio[n] ended with Eisenhower saying, 'We[ll] Brad, those are my orders'.

Thus twenty-four hours after t[he] Verdun decisions, General Bradle[y] found himself deprived of his maj[or] command, Hodges' First Arm[y] which was taking the brunt of th[e] fighting (as Patton had not yet arriv[ed] on the scene). It was now und[er] Montgomery's orders, while h[e] Bradley, had in essence nothing of an[y] significance to do. To this day th[e] mystery endures how Montgomery['s] name was first proposed for th[e] northern command and why Eise[n]hower was to accept him when surel[y] he must have known the controvers[y] the appointment was going to caus[e] But there is no mystery about Gener[al] Bradley's reaction to the change [of] plan.

He was immediately aware that h[is] reputation was at stake and demande[d] that there should be a clear explan[a]tion of why Montgomery had bee[n] given the new command. As he writ[es] in his memoirs: 'For unless th[e] change-over were clearly explained b[y] SHAEF, it could be interpreted as [a] loss of confidence by Eisenhower in m[e] – or more significantly in the Amer[i]can command. If, as a result of th[e]

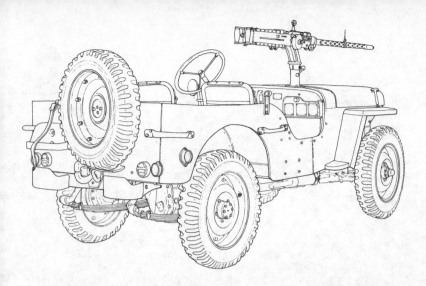

The Willys Jeep was and is probably the most widely used military vehicle of all time. Its importance in winning the war can hardly be overestimated, for it could go virtually anywhere under the most dreadful conditions. Its main advantages were its four wheel drive and a good power-to-weight ratio. It was used as a universal transport, and was often specially equipped with a Browning .5-inch machine gun. *Weight:* 2,750 lbs empty. *Engine:* Willys 4-cylinder inline, 60 bhp. *Fuel:* 13 gallons. *Speed:* 55 mph. *Range:* 225 miles. *Payload:* 3 passengers or 1,200 lbs of other goods (800 lbs cross-country). *Armament:* one .5-inch Browning machine gun

shift, the public were to lose confidence in me, Eisenhower could quickly remedy that situation by sending me home. But if his action were taken to mean repudiation of the American command, if it were inferred that we were bailed out by the British, the damage could be irreparable to our future role in the war'. In this context it must be pointed out that SHAEF did not release the news of the Montgomery appointment till early January 1945 and that for the whole first and more important phase of the Battle of the Bulge, officially Montgomery had nothing to do with the battle. However, the British Press got round the censorship by the old dodge of quoting 'enemy sources' which stated that Montgomery had taken over the northern command.

The reorganisation of the Allied command did not come a moment too soon, for the situation was getting out of hand with General Hodges being

forced even to vacate his own headquarters at Spa because of enemy pressure and the presence of an enemy armored group close at hand. While Hodges' First Army fought a series of delaying actions, the importance of the two vital road and rail centres St Vith and Bastogne grew daily. Due to the lack of roads in the Ardennes and the deep, snow-covered ground, it was imperative that the Germans capture these two towns if they wished to speed their armor to the River Meuse. While Montgomery took over the town of St Vith which was probably the more important of the two centres, Bradley concentrated on the Patton attack from the south, directing at the second town, Bastogne, held by the 101st Airborne.

For the first time in his whole conduct of the 1944-1945 campaign in NW Europe Bradley took a daily and very personal interest in Patton's operations. This can only be explained in

American tank destroyer prepares to repel the German offensive

that he felt he must make his presence known and possibly – perhaps unconsciously – make up for the slur on his reputation occasioned by the Montgomery appointment. For Bradley the relief of Bastogne became a matter of personal prestige. Although he writes in his memoirs that 'in tactical importance that road center (St Vith) was even more valuable than Bastogne itself,' he devotes its defence exactly four sentences in his memoirs – after all St Vith was Montgomery's problem. For Bradley the Battle of the Bulge became inextricably bound up with the defence of Bastogne and Patton's drive towards the beleagured Belgian town. Belittling Hodges' efforts in the north under Montgomery's command: 'Indeed the plight of the First Army had become so grave that unless Patton soon hurried to its aid with a diversion, we feared Hodges' line might crack', he insisted that 'the relief of Bastogne was to be the priority objective in Patton's flanking attack'.

In the end Bastogne was relieved and its relief, perhaps, in part, due to Bradley's insistence on its importance, became one of the most illustrious pages of popular US history. Thereafter Bradley limited his interference in Patton's attempt to link up with Hodges' First Army to a few rare occasions, though even these interventions did not please Patton. 'In one case,' Patton wrote, 'while he did not order, he strongly suggested that instead of attacking north of Diekirch and cutting the enemy off at the waist (as Patton had planned), we should put in a new division southeast of Bastogne so as to insure the integrity of the corridor'.

Patton let himself be 'overpersuaded' (as he put it) and deployed the division – the 90th Infantry – as recommended. The attack did not come off and although Patton assumed responsibility for the failure, he wrote later,

'Had I put the 90th Division in north of Diekirch, I am sure we would have bagged more Germans and just as cheaply'.

A few days later at 0900 hours on 8th January, Bradley intervened again in his plans with a crash project for attacking the vital Belgian town of Houffalize (through which the German armor was escaping) that very same day with the 101st Airborne and the 4th Armored. Patton argued against the project successfully, but next day, Bradley again intervened. This time Patton was ordered in so many words to pull one of his divisions out as a command reserve because Bradley had heard rumours that there might be a German counterattack in the Saar. Two days later Bradley again interfered, advising Patton that a new German attack might materialise somewhere north of Trier.

Although Patton wrote himself: 'These two instances, for which Bradley was personally not responsible, indicate the inadvisability of commanding from too far back,' one cannot overlook the fact that Bradley was responsible for the deeds of his subordinates and that he must have known and approved them. Thus one can only interpret his 'interference' in Patton's campaign in the Ardennes (which was completely uncharacteristic of him) as a reflection of his mood of that time, which Ladislas Farago, Patton's official biographer, characterises as 'brooding at his tactical headquarters'. But, as December gave way to January, Bradley had little time for brooding, then a new threat to his reputation loomed large on the horizon. For it seemed as if Montgomery was attempting to parley his new position as commander of the northern flank of the Bulge into a permanent field command, with both the 21st Army Group and Bradley's 12th Army Group under his control. On the 29th December, he wrote Eisenhower: 'I suggest your directive (concerning the future plans of the Allied armies) should finish with this sentence: "12 and 21 Army Groups will develop operations in accordance with the above instructions. From now onwards full operational direction, control and co-ordination of these operations is vested in C-in-C 21 Army Group subject to such instructions as may be issued by the Supreme Commander from time to time"', . . . 'I put this matter to you again only because I am so anxious not to have another failure'.

The implied insult of the last sentence roused Eisenhower's ire against his frequently insubordinate British subordinate. The long-suffering Supreme Commander wrote back: 'You know how greatly I've appreciated and depended upon your frank and friendly counsel, but in your latest letter you disturb me by predictions of "failure" unless your exact opinions in the matter of giving you command over Bradley are met in detail'.

As soon as Bradley became aware of the threat to his continued independent command, he rushed to Eisenhower to protest, stating his own and his major commanders' opinion of the Montgomery take-over bid. Eisenhower was evasive, and Bradley was forced to state his position unequivocally. 'You must know, Ike,' he told the Supreme Commander, 'that I cannot serve under Montgomery. If he is to be put in command of all ground forces, you must send me home, for if Montgomery goes in over me, I will have lost confidence in my command'.

In his memoirs Bradley then goes on to say that 'Ike flushed. He stiffened in his chair and eyed me hotly'. Instead of supporting his old comrade, it seemed as if he intended to go on with the Montgomery plan. 'Well,' he said, 'I thought you were the one person I could count on for doing anything I asked you to'.

'You can, Ike,' Bradley answered. 'I've enjoyed every bit of my service with you. But this is one thing I cannot take'.

A little while later, Bradley left without a decision having been made.

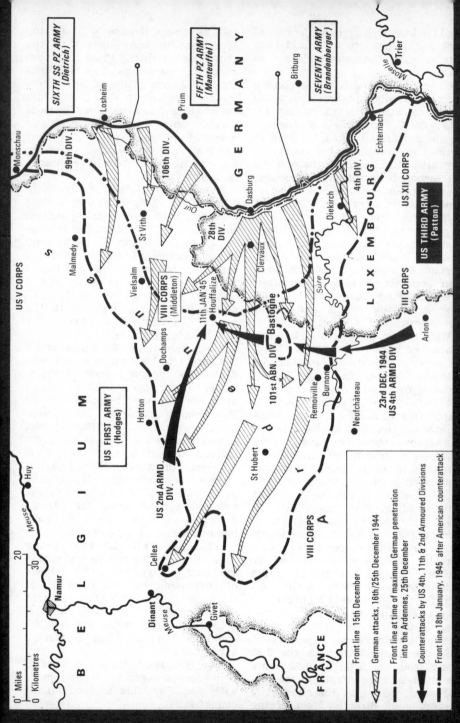

The Battle of the Bulge – the last German offensive in the West

But Bradley's humiliation was not yet complete. On 7th January 1945 after the news had been released that Montgomery had been called to command the northern sector of the Bulge and it was pretty obvious that the German dash for the Meuse was beaten, Montgomery gave a press conference to explain his part in the battle. It was a highly unfortunate decision. In it he described the battle in terms which emphasised his own part in the events of the past three weeks. After describing how the enemy had brought about a situation which 'looked as if it might become awkward,' Montgomery said: 'As soon as I saw what was happening, I took certain steps to ensure that if the Germans got to the Meuse they would certainly not get over that river . . . these were merely precautions, that is, I was thinking ahead'. Continuing in this strain, which gave the impression that Bradley had not been thinking ahead, he said, 'national considerations were thrown overboard'. This was interpreted by the Americans as meaning that the Supreme Commander had called in the best man over the head of the captain of the home team ie Bradley. He followed this by handing out a written statement which praised everyone, Eisenhower, the US generals, the GIs under his command, but overlooked Bradley. Perhaps the omission was unwitting, but it was decidedly unfortunate and with the rest of the Montgomery statement caused an immediate outburst at the Bradley Headquarters in Luxemburg where to make matters worse it was heard in the doctored German version, which Bradley's officers took to be the official BBC version.

Bradley records in his memoirs the reaction of his staff. Hansen (his aide) burst into his office followed by Lieutenant-Colonel Ralph M Ingersoll, editor of New York's now defunct *PM*, and Major Henry E Munson, Lev Allen's young aide.

'You've got to get something on the record,' Hansen said, 'that tells the whole story of this change-over in command. Until you do the American people will have nothing to go by except Montgomery's statement which certainly leaves a questionable inference on the capabilities of the US Command. SHAEF didn't indicate in its statement when the change-over took place and as a result most newspapers have assumed it was made on 17th December. They do not realize that you had the situation well in hand when the change came three days later'. Hansen then handed Bradley a copy of the *Washington Post* for 28th December, in which an editorial demanded the truth about the Ardennes battle, maintaining that 'the American people need an authoritative interpretation of what the Rundstedt offensive is all about'.

The decided opinions of his younger officers, skilled in public relations, convinced Bradley that he must now take the offensive against his British counterpart. However, he was worried that he might not be able to get Eisenhower's permission to make a public statement. 'But you have a precedent,' former press man Ingersoll insisted. 'After all, Montgomery spoke to the press yesterday'.

'Do you suppose Montgomery cleared his interview with Eisenhower?' someone asked.

'You know darned well he didn't!' Bradley exploded.

Two days after the Montgomery statement, Bradley issued his own. It read in part: 'The German attack . . . cut both our direct telephone communications to First Army and the direct roads over which personal contact was normally maintained . . . It was therefore decided that the 21st Army Group should assume temporary command of all Allied forces north of the salient. This was a temporary measure only and when the lines are rejoined 12th Army Group will resume command of all American troops in this area'.

This is an astounding statement. First of all it was contrary to SHAEF

Germany lost many of her most able troops, either killed or captured

policy to have general officers making public statements of this nature (the ban was not taken off till September 1945, i.e. after the war.) Secondly, Bradley had no authority, not even an indication from Eisenhower that Montgomery's appointment was only a temporary one. In fact, on the day that Bradley made it, all indications were that Montgomery was going to be given the permanent control of all Allied ground forces. (Even after the matter was resolved and Montgomery was dismissed, he still retained Simpson's Ninth Army under his control for a further three months).

But the statement indicates two things. Firstly, that General Bradley was surrounded by officers whose devotion to him and antipathy to Montgomery had fogged their objectivity. As John Eisenhower, son of the Supreme Commander, has pointed out: 'If Ralph Ingersoll's account (in *Top Secret*) reflects the prevalent attitude among the 12th Army Group staff, then some of Bradley's advisers were certainly performing their chief a disservice'. Secondly, that the normally retiring commander of the 12th Army Group had finally decided to make a stand against Montgomery, and had, in addition, decided to make this stand publicly (or semi-publicly, relying on the Press to do the rest) in the knowledge that Eisenhower would now be subjected to the pressure of public opinion, not directly of course, but through the person of his boss General Marshall back in Washington, who was acutely sensitive to the wishes of the public and the politicians. Now the fat was well and truly in the fire. The question now was – what was Eisenhower going to do?

A New Year's stocktaking

Since the war there have been many inquests held in an attempt to find out why the American 12th Army Group was tactically surprised in the Ardennes on 16th December 1944. General Bradley has not come out of most of these inquests too well, and it must be admitted that in the final analysis he must – as Army Group Commander – take the overall responsibility for any failing on the part of his subordinates. Yet can one point squarely and honestly at General Bradley and say he was responsible for not foreseeing a German attack which although it ended in an American victory, cost the Americans 80,000 casualties (the largest number of casualties in any single battle or campaign of the whole 1944-1945 war in NW Europe) and definitely put the date of final victory back for at least six weeks?

Naturally the first area of inquiry which comes to mind in this context is that of intelligence. Immediately

after the battle was over, Eisenhower's chief of staff, General Bedell Smith, ordered a secret investigation into the role of intelligence prior to the counterattack: an investigation that was seriously hampered by the fact that SHAEF'S Top Secret Intelligence Digests, of which two copies were supposed to be kept on file, were for some strange reason destroyed. All the evidence and available documents were examined and intelligence cleared. Yet a decade later when writing his official history of the US Army in the Ardennes campaign, Hugh Cole can maintain: 'The prelude to the Ardennes counteroffensive of 16th December can only be reckoned as a gross failure by allied ground and air intelligence'. In the week prior to the start of the German attack, however, Allied intelligence, although hampered by weather so bad that air reconnaissance was limited, was busy, and at least two intelligence officers spotted the build-up in the Ardennes. Indeed some time earlier, in the first week of December 1944, General Strong, Eisenhower's chief of intelligence, had gone to Bradley's headquarters and warned him of the dangers inherent in his thinly held Ardennes front. And in the post-war years Forest Pogue, also of the official US history staff, could point out: 'One might well ask what additional information the Allies would have needed to predict the 16th December attack. In many ways their information was highly accurate . . . Despite the clever deceptive measures of the enemy, the Allied intelligence experts had correctly analyzed most of the German dispositions and in the closing hours before the counteroffensive, were aware of the shifts toward the Ardennes area and of the arrival of new units in the zone of VIII Corps'.

Perhaps the answer to the enigma of why the warnings of some of the intelligence men were not taken seriously is a compound of two things: the

A tank destroyer prepares for action in the Battle of the Bulge

general heady optimism of the time among senior Allied officers; and the strangely 'anti-intelligence' attitude of General Bradley's own chief intelligence officer General Edwin Sibert. Sibert, a relatively new man in the field, was by nature inclined to scepticism. In addition he was at loggerheads with the more experienced First Army's chief of intelligence, Colonel 'Monk' Dickson, who two days before the start of the offensive had predicted: 'Reinforcements for the West Wall between Düren and Trier continue to arrive. The identification of at least three or four newly reformed divisions along the army front must be reckoned with during the next few days . . . it is possible that a limited scale offensive will be launched for purpose of achieving a Christmas morale victory for civilian consumption. Many PWs now speak of the coming attack between the 17th and 25th December'.

Although Colonel Dickson predicted the offensive would probably come just north of Middleton's stretch of the line (where the attack actually take place), the point of attack was close enough to the thinly held Ardennes to have caused concern if it had not been for the scepticism of his superior Sibert.(Three days later when Dickson saw Sibert after the start of the offensive he could not refrain from rubbing his nose in the dirt and remarking that his last intelligence bulletin would tell Sibert all he needed to know about the German intention). However Sibert refused to pass on Dickson's or any other intelligence officer's fears about the 12th Army Group to General Bradley. In fact, he encouraged his superior in the belief, which one must point out was held by other senior allied commanders including General Montgomery, that the enemy would not attack. After the war General Bradley could write honestly in his memoirs that 'No one came to me with a warning on the danger of a counterattack there (the Ardennes)', and 'it was impossible for

me even to scan the intelligence estimates of subordinate units'.

Then, if intelligence was not to blame for the failure of the 12th Army Group to predict the German attack, who was? One could say naturally the Army commander on whose front the break-through took place and whose intelligence officer predicted a possible German attack, namely General Hodges of the US First Army. In his memoirs Bradley seems to point the finger indirectly at his subordinate when he writes: 'As though to compensate for the indignity it suffered when First Army was forced to evacuate its CP at Spa during the Bulge, that staff afterwards excerpted its record to "prove" First Army had been clairvoyant in predicting the German offensive, but that its "predictions" had been disregarded at higher headquarters – meaning Army Group? 'First Army's contention is pure nonsense for it was just as neatly hoodwinked by Rundstedt as was the rest of the Allied command. While I freely accept responsibility for our "calculated risk" in the Ardennes, I do not admit that there were any significant warnings given me which I chose to ignore'.

But this 'calculated risk', which Bradley admits to, directly involved Hodges, for it meant that Bradley undertook to strengthen his southern (Patton) drive and his northern one (Hodges) at the expense of the Ardennes front, where an extremely ragged front of some sixty miles was held by four divisions, two completely green and two badly battered in previous fighting. As Bradley himself writes: 'Instead of employing our surplus divisions in the quiet Ardennes we used them to attack in other sectors'. It is, therefore, worth while examining this 'calculated risk' which General Bradley admits to and which gave the Germans the opportunity for offensive action they were looking for.

As Bradley himself states, the 'calculated risk' was valid because it freed divisions for action elsewhere and

Generals Hodges, Montgomery, Bradley and Dempsey meet to confer

consequently it was only to remain valid while active operations continued. But by the first week of December 1944, however, the main American drive across the German frontier had come to an abrupt halt. As a result German reserves were freed for the Ardennes counter-offensive. But at the same time American divisions should also have been freed to meet the potential threat in the Ardennes, for, although Patton was to launch an attack in the Saar in the third week of December, Hodges had, at Bradley's orders, no intention of attacking again until the second week in January. Accordingly the concentration of American troops around the Aachen area in mid-December served no particular purpose whatsoever.

In addition, if Bradley regarded the thinly held Ardennes front as a 'calculated risk', one must assume he also had a contingency plan up his sleeve in case the Germans attacked in that area. But what happened when the Germans actually did attack? At

Eisenhower's suggestion he ordered two armoured divisions from the flanking armies to support Middleton. This was on the first evening of the attack, as we have seen. Thereafter it took another twenty-four hours before SHAEF's sole reserves (i.e.not Bradley's), the two battered airborne divisions, were ordered into the Ardennes. Another twelve hours passed before Patton was ordered to call off his Saar attack. Three days after the start of the German attack, he had still not started drawing appreciable forces from the Roer front to aid Hodges; and after four days he had still not produced an overall plan to meet the threat. By then Montgomery was in charge of the northern sector.

In short, the 'calculated risk' that General Bradley refers to must have been a post-Ardennes invention, a convenient excuse for his lack of preparation for the German attack. This

81

sounds a harsh judgment on a fine soldier, but its impact is immediately lessened when it is understood that General Bradley shared the widespread feeling of December 1944 that the Germans were finished and it was now only a matter of time before they were beaten. Admittedly their final defeat was not so assured as it had been in August 1944. There might still be some hard fighting as the Allies penetrated into the Rhineland, but one thing was sure – the Germans would never again be able to launch a counter-offensive!

All the writers (including General Bradley himself) who have sought to excuse his apparent failure in the Ardennes and who have confused the issue considerably by 'passing the buck,' by accusing some other senior commander or even by regarding the Ardennes as a kind of victory for Bradley, have overlooked to greater or lesser degree the heady optimistic mood of the time which encouraged senior commanders to believe what

they wanted to believe and not what the hard military facts should have told them to believe. One of the earliest chroniclers of the Battle of the Bulge, who was present during the operations, summed up the mood of the time as follows: 'Despite the crushing, grinding fighting of October and November, optimism, which reached its height during the chase across France, continued to pervade all ranks of the Anglo-American armies, sometimes to the blinding of reason . . . the underestimation of the German ability to recover was the most flagrant example of this overoptimism . . . Those were certainly days of smug satisfaction when people felt that the glorious days of victory could not be far off . . . We were lured to sleep by the lilting music of Hitler's muses, as we had been before at Pearl

Harbor, and once again we were saved, this time not only by our resilience and ability to bound back from a shock, but also by the real weakness of the German arms. But we should have learned from these lessons. As it was, it might have been the spring of 1940 all over again'.

But by January 1945 the damage had been done. Now a mood had been engendered in Bradley's headquarters, firstly, by the Montgomery appointment and interview of 7th January, secondly, by Eisenhower's pre-occupation with the possibility of Montgomery taking over the whole of the field armies, and, thirdly, the feeling that Bradley had failed, which was going to colour the rest of the NW European campaign. From now onwards, I do not think it would be unfair to say that the main enemy for the officers around Bradley was no longer the German, but Field-Marshal Montgomery and to some extent Eisenhower, or at least his SHAEF intimates.

As we have seen already Bradley had already made his position known publicly about the possibility of Montgomery's appointment to the control of all land forces. The result was encouraging. The American press supported his attitude. Churchill telephoned Eisenhower to ask the latter to convey his personal apologies to Bradley on the way the British press had handled the Ardennes aftermath, the Montgomery interview, and his own interviews with the journalists accredited to SHAEF. A few days later the British Prime Minister got up in the house and praised Bradley's command of the 12th Army Group during the counter-offensive. Support also began to come from the Chiefs of Staff back in Washington and Eisenhower gave way to the extent of returning Hodges' First Army to Bradley's command, but leaving Simpson's Ninth under Montgomery's control.

Supplies are air-dropped
in Bastogne under heavy
attack

Left: US forces move north to cut the wedge of the German winter offensive. *Above:* US armour moves south to restore the Ardennes to the Allies

Now Bradley, eager to regain his lost prestige and ensure that Montgomery should not extend his hold on American troops, sprang out of the 'brooding mood' which several officers attest he was afflicted by at that time. Actively encouraged by many of his senior staff, he directed his efforts so that Eisenhower would be forced to grant him an important role in the operations to come, with the emphasis in his statements to Eisenhower being that national considerations must have a definite place in future operations. The US Army had appeared to have suffered a setback in the Ardennes and with it their commander Bradley. Now it was up to Eisenhower to ensure that he, Bradley, must have an opportunity to overcome that particular stigma.

Lieutenant-Colonel Ingersoll, who encouraged Bradley to reply to the Montgomery statement of 7th January 1945, and who is a man who reveals himself, in his book on the campaign published immediately after the war – *Top Secret*, to be almost pathologically anti-British, writes: 'Until the Ardennes, Bradley and his officers had made an honest attempt to deal fairly and frankly with the British, to work together in open convenants openly arrived at. After the Ardennes, no one was ever frank with anyone. Fair, there was a scrupulous effort to be – almost a doubling over backwards; but frank, never. Bradley – and Patton, Hodges, and Simpson under Bradley's direction – proceeded to make and carry out their plans without the assistance of official command channels, on a new basis openly discussed only among themselves. This basis squarely faced the facts that in order to defeat the enemy, by direct attack and in the shortest possible time, they had 1. to conceal their plans from the British, and 2.

Above: American airborne troops, besieged in Bastogne, move out to counterattack. *Left:* Troops move through the wooded Ardennes during the Allied advance

almost literally outwit Eisenhower's Supreme Headquarters, half of which was British and the other half of which was beyond their power to influence by argument. They completely succeeded in both objectives and won the war'.

While Bradley thus prepared to secure his position in future operations even at the risk of an open break with the British ally, Eisenhower now prepared to launch his drive for the Rhine. He intended to make the main drive to the north because once the Rhine was crossed, he envisaged Montgomery playing the leading part in the attack on the Reich itself north of the Ruhr. In addition to this, Bradley would make a complementary attack from the Mainz-Frankfurt area north east of Kassel. This would result in 'a massive double envelopment of the Ruhr to be followed by a great thrust

to join with the Russians'. However, before this could be done the armies of the enemy west of the Rhine had to be dealt with. When this plan was presented to the British Chiefs of Staff in January, they objected that Eisenhower would never have enough strength to do more than 'mount one full-blooded attack across the Rhine'. This latter should be to the north and as a consequence Eisenhower should 'pass to the defensive on all other parts of the line'.

Eisenhower did not agree. Perhaps he was already aware what the impact of the single thrust north of the Rhine would have on Bradley and American public opinion. He passed on the argument to Marshall, who in the end solved the problem by stating categoriaclly that if the Eisenhower plan were not accepted by the British generals, he would 'recommend to Eisenhower that he had no choice but to ask to be relieved of his command'. As a result Eisenhower was now able to present the three phases of his Rhineland plan to his subordinates Bradley and Montgomery:

Phase One: Montgomery was to seize the west bank of the Rhine from Nijmegen to Düsseldorf. During this period of time Bradley's forces were to maintain an aggressive defence.

Phase Two: While Montgomery prepared to cross the Rhine by one of his set-piece battles, Bradley was to secure the Rhine west bank from Düsseldorf to Koblenz. This would be carried out by the First Army striking for Cologne while the Third headed for Koblenz through the Eifel.

Phase Three: While Montgomery crossed the Rhine, the US Third and Seventh Armies would clean out the Moselle-Saar triangle and secure bridgeheads on the Mainz-Karlsruhe sector ready for the southern envelopment of the Ruhr.

Although the fact that Marshall had turned down the single thrust to the Rhine advocated by the British, meant that Montgomery would not be the overall ground force commander,

German POWs; but there were 80,000 US casualties

Bradley was not satisfied with the Eisenhower plan. But then why should he be? For, at its face value, it meant that Montgomery would keep the Ninth Army, that other American armies would be used in operations that would bring credit to Montgomery and not to himself, and that Ridgway's XVIII Airborne Corps would be retained by Montgomery for the set-piece Lower Rhine crossing.

Bradley suggested an alternative plan. According to his way of thinking the main thrust towards the Rhine should be carried out by his First and Third Armies and straight through the Eifel to the Cologne-Koblenz area. This would mean that offensive operations in the Reich itself would be in central Germany and that if there were only going to be one thrust into the heart of the country it would be made by Bradley's men with Montgomery's 21st Army Group playing nothing more than a flanking role in

the north. Although Bradley pointed out that his plan was motivated not merely by military considerations but also national ones (he told one of Eisenhower's staff that if SHAEF wanted 'to destroy the whole operation', they could 'do so and be damned' and that 'much more than a tactical operation was involved in that the prestige of the American Army was at stake.'), it was turned down by the Supreme Commander.

As it looked at the beginning of February 1945 Bradley was committed to the Eifel campaign leading him to the Rhine, and to be followed by Montgomery's major crossing of the river barrier. The latter would, therefore, gain the kudos of the major victory in the heart of the Reich as his forces sped easily through the open plains of Westphalia towards the Elbe and perhaps from there to Berlin itself. But in the next eight weeks a great deal was to change in the overall plan – and change to the advantage of the hurt, and now highly sensitive, American commander.

Attack to the Rhine

On the 4th of February, General Patton, whose Third Army was now attempting to force the Germans on its front into the Eifel, received a call from General Bradley. 'Monty did it again, George,' Bradley said. 'You and Hodges will go on the defensive while Montgomery will resume the offensive in the north'. Anticipating Patton's usual explosive reaction, he continued hastily. 'It wasn't Ike this time. Orders from the Combined Chiefs. Brooke (Sir Alan, British CIGS) even got General Marshall to go along with him. I don't know what made him agree. Probably he's anxious to get those fourteen British divisions sitting on their butts in Belgium back into action'.

'What are they hoping to accomplish?' Patton asked.

'Montgomery wants to secure a wide stretch of the Rhine as quickly as possible,' the 12th Army Group commander replied, 'so that we would have a quick entry if Germany collapsed suddenly'.

'Horsefeathers!' was Patton's reply. 'I'm convinced that we have a much better chance to get to the Rhine first with our present attack. When are the British supposed to jump off'?

'Probably on the 10th'.

'I doubt if Monty will be ready by the 10th,' Patton said. 'But what are we supposed to be doing in the meantime'?

'You can continue your attack until February 10th, and maybe even after that provided your casualties aren't excessive and you have enough ammunition left'.

Infected by Bradley's new attitude to Montgomery and SHAEF, Patton, thereupon started to interpret Eisenhower's concept of 'active defense' during Phase One of the Rhineland campaign in his own way. Shortly after the conversation with Bradley, he revealed his plans for the continuation of the Eifel campaign in the following terms:

'For this offensive [the Rhine], the Field-Marshal is to get nine United States infantry and several armoured divisions ... Third Army will be required to transfer several divisions to Ninth Army. We will get the bad news later. Whatever it is, we will comply promptly and without argument. However, it is very obvious now who is running this war over here and how it is being run.

'Personally I think that it would be a foolish and ignoble way for the Americans to end the war by sitting on our butts. And gentlemen, we aren't going to do anything foolish or ignoble'.

Making it obvious in this manner that he was going to disobey orders, Patton decided to attack Prum and and Bitburg in the Eifel (both well-defended small towns which would necessitate heavy fighting later on), keeping his intentions secret from anyone save General Bradley, then, as he told his staff, 'Let the gentlemen up

US tanks cross the Moselle under a smokescreen

north learn what we are doing when they see it on their maps'.

Just short of three weeks later and well past General Bradley's deadline of 10th February for the end of his Eifel Campaign, Patton again conferred with his boss. This time Bradley gave him full details of the Eisenhower plan for the Rhineland campaign. Patton soon realised that his army was to play the weakest role in it. Almost casually he asked Bradley: 'It is my understanding that I have the authority to push the attack of the Third Army east to secure the Kyll river as extended south by the deep gorge generally ten kilometers east of the crossings over the Saar river; and furthermore, if opportunity presents itself for a quick breakthrough by armour supported by motorised infantry to the Rhine river, then I have the authority to take advantage of that situation?'

Bradley, eager to seize an opportunity which would help to throw the balance of the attack to the Rhine from the north into his own sphere of command, realised Patton's intention immediately: 'Of course. You would have to exploit any opportunity like that.'

Thus as February began to give way to March and Montgomery had still not reached the Rhine, the Third Army, which had been assigned the minor role in the campaign, was creeping deeper into Germany with Bradley's active connivance. On 9th March, Patton was falsely informed that his troops had captured a bridge across the Moselle. Thereupon, he got permission from Eisenhower to exploit the capture. A little later he learned that the bridge was not in American hands. Again Patton acted decisively and presumably contrary to the overall plan. He ordered his staff to cut the lines to 'higher authorities' till further notice and then ordered his corps commander, Eddy, to get as many bridges across the river as were needed and continue the advance.

Meanwhile Hodges' First Army's official campaign was getting in its stride. On 5th March, the northern corps of the First Army reached Cologne and found the Rhine without a bridge there. In the next two days a dozen Rhine bridges went crashing into the mighty water barrier between Koblenz and Duisburg, and every attempt at seizing a bridge, such as that at Düsseldorf, by *coup de main*, had ended in failure. Then on 7th March, General Hoge's Combat Command of the 9th Armored Division reached the river twenty-five miles downstream of Cologne and saw to their amazement that the railway bridge at Remagen was not yet blown. Located on a steep ridge overlooking the Ludendorff Bridge, the Americans learned from a prisoner that the bridge was to be blown at four. The time was was now ten minutes after three. The GIs did not hesitate. By ten minutes to four they were down on the waterfront on the western end of the bridge. Frantically the Germans at the other end tried to blow the already bomb-damaged structure. American engineers ran around wildly cutting every demolition cable they could see. Now the infantry stormed the bridge. A charge went off. Then another. The bridge shuddered, but held. The main charge failed to go off. And then the Americans were over and the bridge was theirs. General Hoge acted quickly and contrary to orders (for he had been commanded to swing south and head for Koblenz). He poured reinforcements across, who formed a shallow but viable bridgehead beyond the eastern end of the bridge. By dusk the Ludendorff Bridge was well and truly in US hands, one of the greatest single achievements of the whole campaign and totally unexpected.

Bradley was conferring with General Bull, Eisenhower's G-3, when he heard the news of the surprise capture. He told General Hodges 'to shove everything you can across and button the bridgehead up tightly'. Then he told Bull. Bull was not impressed. He told Bradley that the general plan

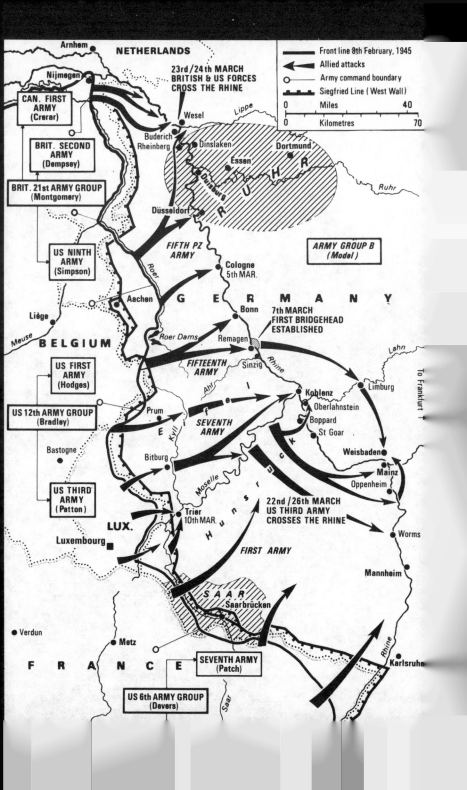

Left: **Pershing tanks during the Allied dash for the Rhine.** *Above:* **US troops move forward along congested roads intent on reaching the Rhine first**

envisaged no place for the Remagen Bridge, especially as the terrain on the eastern bank of the Rhine at Remagen was difficult and hilly, and decidedly not very suitable for armored exploitation. Bradley angrily asked Bull if he wanted Hodges to blow the bridge up and withdraw, then called Eisenhower.

Eisenhower was delighted with the news. He told Bradley, 'Hold on to it, Brad. Get across with whatever you need – but make certain you hold that bridgehead'.

But at dinner later that day, Bull was still unimpressed. 'You know our plans for the Rhine crossing,' he told Bradley, referring to the Montgomery plan as the major large scale crossing to the north, 'And now you're trying to change them'.

'Change hell, Pink!' Bradley snapped. 'We're not trying to change a thing. But now that we've had a break on the bridge, I want to take advantage of it'. General Bull did not believe that Bradley was not really seeking a diversion of forces from Montgomery, which would be needed if the Remagen bridgehead were to be properly exploited. 'Ike's heart is in your sector,' he told Bradley, 'but right now his mind is up north'.

But although Eisenhower's mind might have been up north (with Montgomery), it was still not made up, for he was not to reach his final decision on whether there should be a single or double thrust across the Rhine until the 15th March. Now with the First Army having achieved a bridgehead on the river and Patton coming up rapidly through the Eifel on the left bank of the Moselle towards Koblenz, Bradley thought he saw a chance to give his own troops a chance to play at least an equal role with those commanded by Montgomery. On the day after Eisenhower had told

Above: The only one left standing; Remagen bridge on the Rhine. *Below:* Remagen bridge in Allied hands; Bradley's and Patton's answer to Montgomery's carefully prepared 'bounce'. *Right:* The Germans got to Cologne bridge first

US engineers straddle the Rhine after the switch to a southern Allied offensive

YOU ARE NOW
CROSSING THE
RHINE RIVER
THROUGH COURTESY
OF E CO. 17 ARMD.
ENGR. BN. AND
'C' CO. 202
ENGR. C. BN.

im to 'get across with whatever you eed', SHAEF ordered him to limit is commitment to no more than four ivisions. Bradley could see the riting on the wall. Now he was pprehensive that the First Army's emagen bridgehead might not be xploited after all. With the Ninth US rmy already earmarked for Montomery's thrust into the Ruhr and the ossibility of further divisions going to he same command, Bradley realised hat his command might be whittled own so drastically that the doublencirclement of the Ruhr would be ndangered. He knew that once Montomery had crossed the Rhine, his ivisions would be drawn away from im to support the Englishman. Hence was imperative that he should get nvolved in further bridgeheads across he Rhine as soon as possible so that isenhower would find it impossible o take troops away from him. At a onference on 9th March, he revealed is concern to his army commanders, [odges and Patton. Afterwards the tter wrote: 'We all felt it was ssential that the First and Third rmies should get themselves so nvolved that Montgomery's plan to se most of the divisions on the Vestern Front, British and American, nder his command for an attack on he Ruhr plains, could not come off nd the First and Third Armies be eft out on a limb'.

Accordingly, Bradley again decided o give Patton his head. The fiery hird Army commander needed no rging. Without hesitation he acepted Bradley's suggestion that he hould cross the Lower Moselle, southest of Koblenz, try to penetrate the ugged Hunsruck mountains with his rmor and head for the Rhine between Iainz and Mannheim. Here he was, to se Montgomery's term of the previous eptember, to 'bounce the Rhine' and ry to establish an additional bridgeead to that created by Hodges at

Remagen before the 'master of the set piece battle' had even started on his well-planned Rhine crossing. On 14th March, Patton launched his attack. Within two days his armor had fought its way through the extremely difficult and easily defended Hunsruck and turned the corner of the Rhine into the rolling plain leading to the Mainz-Mannheim area. Spurred on continually by Bradley's warning that Montgomery was hot for his divisions, Patton roared closer and closer to the river, giving his corps and divisional commanders no chance to hesitate.

On the 19th, Patton beat off a German counter-attack. That same evening he was within ten miles from Mainz. Hard at his heels came his bridging equipment, which he had dragged with him ever since the Ardennes for just this occasion. That day Bradley urged him to 'take the Rhine on the run'. Now Patton had only four days before Montgomery launched his great Rhine crossing. The question was now – where would Patton cross the river?

At Mainz there was an estimated brigade of SS soldiers on the far bank, waiting for an expected US crossing there. Patton reacted by blanketing the river at that point with thick artificial fog and during the night of 22/23rd slipped six battalions of the US 5th Infantry Division across the Rhine at the little town of Oppenheim. The surprise was complete. General Irwin had the whole of his 5th Division across by the following morning at a cost of some eight men killed and twenty wounded. The surprise was total and although the enemy reacted violently when he realised how he had been tricked, throwing in the last of his jet fighters in order to wipe out the bridgehead, Patton stuck to his gain like glue. He had beaten Montgomery by a day.

When Lieutenant-Colonel Stillman, Patton's liaison officer at 12th Group's HQ, submitted his report on the new Rhine crossing, his attitude reflected the attitude of everyone present and

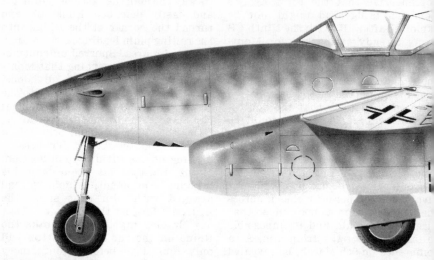

their delight in the way that the Army Group had stolen a march on Montgomery. With a grin on his face the young liaison officer said: 'Without benefit of aerial bombing, ground smoke, artillery preparation and airborne assistance [all thought very necessary by Montgomery preparing for his crossing further north], the Third Army at 2200 hours, Thursday evening, March 22, crossed the Rhine River'. (It is rumoured that Patton wanted to make fun of Montgomery's elaborate Rhine airborne operation, involving two divisions, by ferrying individual infantrymen across the Rhine at Oppenheim by means of Third Army spotter planes.) That same evening Patton emphasised the real importance of the new Rhine crossing by his excited telephone call to Bradley in which he shouted: 'Brad, for God's sake tell the world we're across. We knocked down thirty-three Krauts today when they came after our pontoon bridges. I want the world to know Third Army made it before Monty starts across!'

Bradley's tactical improvisation in the Eifel and central Rhinelan[d] which in its way was brilliant bu[t] motivated by personal and nation[al] considerations rather than strateg[ic] ones, now paid handsome dividend[s]. In the third week of March Eisenhowe[r] decided that the additional division[s] from Bradley's command, which ha[d] been earmarked for Montgomery[']s northern thrust should now remain i[n] the centre. He also came to the co[n]clusion that as more reserves becam[e] available, they would be given t[o] Bradley, and not to Montgomery, s[o] that he could swiftly complete th[e] planned encirclement of the Ruhr an[d] then head east to link up with th[e] Russians. As a result he could no[w] order Bradley to move all three Firs[t] Army corps across the Rhine a[t] Remagen.

On the 24th, the First Army starte[d] to cross the river and instead o[f] striking north towards the Ruhr, a[s] the enemy was anticipating, heade[d] east along the valley of the River Sie[g] and south-east towards the Rive[r] Lahn to link up with Patton's Thir[d] Army which was forming new bridge[s]

The Messerschmidt Me 262 *Schwalbe* was the world's first operational turbojet-driven fighter. The type was very advanced aerodynamically for its time, *Engines:* two Junkers Jumo 004B-1 turbojets, 1,980 lbs static thrust each *Armament:* four 30-mm MK 108 cannon with 360 rounds plus 24 R4M air to air missiles. *Speed:* 540 mph at 19,684 feet. *Initial climb rate:* 3,937 feet per minute. *Ceiling:* 37,565 feet. *Range:* 652 miles at 29,560 feet. *Weight empty/loaded:* 9,741/14,101 lbs. *Span:* 40 feet 11½ inches. *Length:* 34 feet 9½ inches

heads over the Rhine between Mainz and Koblenz.

For three days the Germans managed to hold this development, but on 28th March Patton and Hodges, who had joined up at Giessen, broke loose and drove forward in a great sweep down the Frankfurt-Kassel corridor in a great curving sweep which was to take them east of the Ruhr. Meanwhile Simpson's Ninth Army, still under Montgomery, swept forward on the other side of the Ruhr till on the 1st April 1945 Simpson's 2nd Armored Division and Hodges' 3rd Armored linked up at the little medieval town of Lippstadt. In one bold move Field-Marshal Model's Army Group of over 350,000 men were trapped in the Ruhr, an area of some sixty miles by forty.

Now Bradley's standing and position with Eisenhower had changed drastically since those late January days when the three-phase Rhineland campaign had allotted him a relatively minor role in the operations. The two armies under his command had fought an exciting and dramatic campaign against the bulk of the German forces in the west, which had culminated in the thrilling and unexpected capture of two bridgeheads across the Rhine, while Montgomery had plodded on drearily and undramatically to a Rhine crossing which, in the final analysis, was not much more than an anti-climax. After his apparent failure in the Ardennes, Bradley was now at the top of his form and standing high in Eisenhower's book. As the latter told his aide Commander Butcher about this period of Bradley's leadership: 'Bradley has never held back and never has "paused to regroup" when he saw an opportunity to advance'. The implied criticism contained in the term 'paused to re-group' was obvious: it was aimed directly at Montgomery. The time had come for the Supreme Commander to do some serious re-thinking on the subject of the attack into the heart of Germany and the commander who would have the task of leading that attack which would bring him the honour of the final victory over the Nazi enemy.

Debris from the retreating German army hinders the US Third Army's advance

The Elbe
decisions

On the afternoon of 28th March, Eisenhower sat at his desk in his office at the *École Professionelle et Technique des Garçons*, Rheims, preparing three telegrams. One was addressed to General Marshall in Washington; one to Premier Churchill in London; one, the most important of all, marked 'Personal to Marshal Stalin', to Moscow.

On that day, General Eisenhower revealed his plan of campaign for the final attack on Germany to the Soviet leader a thousand miles or so away in Moscow. With his armies now successfully across the Rhine, he proposed to make his main thrust along the axis Erfurt-Leipzig-Dresden, and there to link up with the Red Army advancing from the East. This accomplished he intended driving his left wing (Montgomery) north-east to Hamburg and the Baltic and his right (Patton) south-east to meet the Russians in the valley of the Danube.

It was a simple honest explanation of his strategy and when he was finished with his telegrams 'Ike', as millions called him all over the world, was pretty sure that 'UJ' (short for 'Uncle Joe') would be pleased with the plan. Yet that simple message, sent in good faith from one ally to another, was later to be regarded as perhaps the most momentous decision of the whole war for it meant that two US armies – the Ninth and First – would halt at the Elbe and the glittering prize of Berlin', as Eisenhower himself had once called the German capital, was to be left to the Russians.

The new American plan had an instant and angry reaction in London. Both the British Chiefs of Staff and Churchill protested at the high-handed manner in which Eisenhower had informed Stalin of his intentions and more importantly at the fact that he was prepared to allow the Russians to take Berlin. But Eisenhower, confident that he had the backing of Marshall, who in this last month of the ailing President Roosevelt's life was virtually running the war, stuck to his guns. If the British wished a showdown over this issue he was prepared to give them it. The next day he cabled Marshall: 'I have always insisted that the northern attack would be the principal effort (Montgomery's command) in that phase of our operations that involves the isolation of the Ruhr, but from the very beginning, extending back before D-Day my plan . . . has been to link up the primary and secondary efforts in the Kassel area and then make one great thrust to the eastward.'

He then went on to explain that this thrust was now being made in the direction of Dresden and not Berlin because the former contained 'The greater part of the remaining German industrial capacity' and was the area 'to which the German Ministries are believed to be moving'.

In the ensuing battle with Churchill over the controversial decision Marshall supported his protégé fully and Eisenhower was able to go ahead with his plan. This was to give Montgomery's 21st Army Group not much more than 'a flanking role', as an angry Churchill was to put it, while Bradley's armies carried out the last major offensive action of the war.

Since the war several reasons have been advanced to explain Eisenhower's sudden and decisive change, which resulted in such a drastic alteration to the face of Europe. There are those who excuse his action by maintaining that his hands were tied and he could not advance over the Elbe because of some 'secret deal' made at Yalta Conference of February 1945. But, contrary to popular belief, the conference at the Crimean coastal resort did not cut Europe up into 'spheres of influence'. It is true that an area of Germany had been designated as that of the Soviet Zone of occupation. But it was never proposed,

Himmler visits the eastern front to encourage the German armies

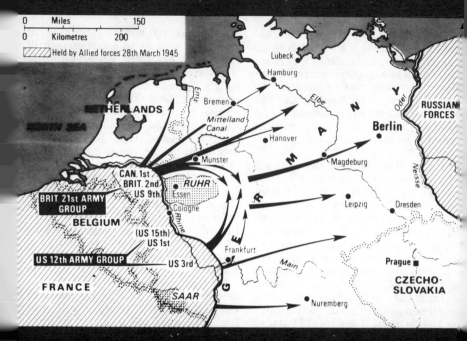

Miles 0 150
Kilometres 0 200

In September 1944, Eisenhower's plan called for a major thrust to Berlin by Montgomery's 21st Army Group. US 12th Army Group would therefore play a secondary role

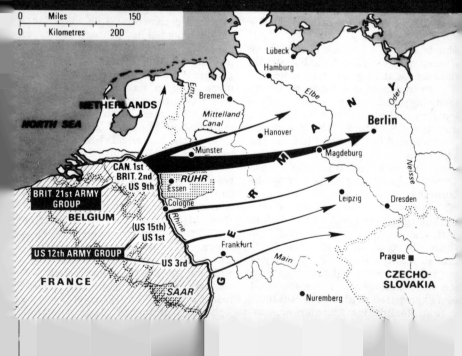

much less agreed upon, that the Anglo-American armies coming from the west should not enter this proposed zone. If the western Allies were going to be in a position to take Berlin, there was no agreement, secret or otherwise, which stopped them doing so. As Churchill wrote later: 'It was well understood by everyone that the agreed occupational zones must not hamper the operational movements of the armies. Berlin, Prague and Vienna could be taken by whoever got there first'.

Was it for a military reason then that Eisenhower did not strike for Berlin? In his own justification of his action, the Supreme Commander quotes General Bradley as advising him that Berlin might cost the Allies '100,000 casualties... to break through from the Elbe to Berlin,' and this was a 'pretty stiff price to pay for a prestige objective. Especially when we've got to fall back and let the other fellow (i.e. the Russians) take over'.

Forrest C Pogue, the great Eisenhower apologist, supports this view. He writes: 'It is evident that the political leaders in the US had framed no policy for dealing with an aggressive Soviet Union and Central Europe. It is equally clear that no political directive was ever issued to General Eisenhower . . . It is evident from the messages that he received from Washington that military solutions were preferred. In this situation the Supreme Commander reached his decisions relative to Berlin and Prague on military rather than political grounds . . . When considered from the purely military viewpoint of the quickest way to end the war in Germany with the fewest number of casualties to our troops, leaving the maximum number available for rapid redeployment to the Pacific, his decision was certainly the proper one'.

But was this true? Would Berlin have cost the Allies so many casualties? When Eisenhower made his decision Montgomery, who would have led the attack to Berlin, was some 200 miles away from the capital, the Russians less than forty. Yet that March it was obvious that the heart had gone out of the German defenders in the West, who had not one single strong natural defensive position till the Elbe. On the Russian front, on the other hand, the Germans had been able to establish strong defensive positions on the Oder and Neisse. From the Baltic to Czechoslovakia, the Germans were bitterly defending every square metre of ground. In Hungary the Russians were blocked too. If the Germans in the West had lost heart after the Ardennes offensive, they were still prepared to contest the Russians in the East with every last bit of strength.

Some indication of the différent types of opposition encountered on the two fronts is revealed by the fact that Allied division often rolled twenty and thirty miles a day against token opposition with negligible casualties (the US 2nd Armored Division, for instance, dashed seventy-three road miles in just under twenty-four hours). It took the Allies only thirteen days to get to the Elbe after the decision of 28th March, while the Russians were still not within long-range artillery distance of Berlin in spite of their having suffered many thousands of casualties.

Militarily, it can be assumed, that Eisenhower had as good a chance of taking Berlin that spring as his Soviet counterpart Marshal Zhukov. In fact, he probably had a better one with the possibility of far fewer casualties at the hands of an enemy who would have been only too glad to see eastern Germany occupied by the western allies rather than the hated Russians.

In the years that he stood for president and had to face severe criticism on account of his Elbe decision from his political enemies, notably from his ex-boss General McArthur, Eisenhower offered another justification for his action: the problem of the 'Alpine Redoubt', an area of Bavaria and Austria, concentrated around the

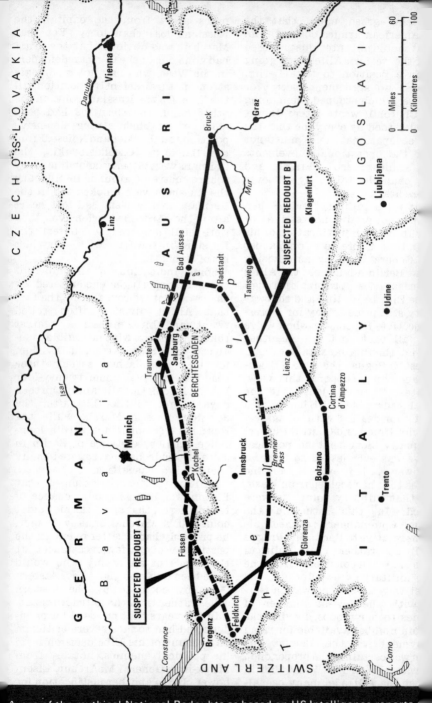

Areas of the mythical National Redoubts as based on US Intelligence reports a
Swiss Newspapers

Alps, and supposedly defended by a fanatical group of elite Nazi troops.

The stories of the mythical redoubt started to find their way into the Swiss papers in late '44 and were picked up and reproduced by American newspapers and journals the following January. In its last issue for that month, the US magazine *Colliers*, for instance, ran an article giving an extremely detailed picture of a gigantic guerilla warfare programme to be run from the 'National Redoubt' under the leadership of the scarfaced Nazi police general Ernst Kaltenbrunner, who was known to be in the area. Naturally Allied intelligence looked into the matter, actively aided by OSS chief agent Alan Dulles. In the 11th March issue of his 'Weekly Intelligence Summary', Major-General Kenneth Strong, Eisenhower's chief of intelligence wrote: 'The main trend of German defense policy does seem directed primarily to the safeguarding of the Alpine zone. This area is by the very nature of the terrain practically impenetrable. The evidence indicates that considerable numbers of SS and specially chosen units are being systematically withdrawn to Austria – and that some of the most important ministires and personalities of the Nazi regime are already established in the Redoubt area'. Strong followed up this statement by one a little later in which he stated: 'Emphasis (should) be placed on offensives to interfere with rumoured enemy plans to build a National Redoubt in the mountainous area running from western Austria as far as the lakes below Munich and as far south as the Italian lakes'.

Finally the 'National' or 'Alpine Redoubt' concept reached General Marshall back in Washington. On 27th March, he wrote Eisenhower advising him to change his direction of attack towards Munich 'to prevent the enemy from organizing resistance in southern Germany'. On that same day too, Eisenhower also received a message from Field-Marshal Montgomery in which he spelled out his plans for the next few weeks. In nine terse paragraphs, he told Eisenhower that he intended 'to drive hard for the Elbe' and finally 'by autobahn to Berlin, I hope'.

The Montgomery message made Eisenhower react 'like a horse with a burr under his saddle'. Montgomery was proving as intractable as ever. His cable read like a demand and not the request it should be, as it was addressed to a superior officer. Montgomery was intent on gaining the credit for the final victory for himself and, to boot, using a great American Army, the Ninth, to help him do so.

Perhaps it was these two messages, both received on the day he made his fatal decision, that acted as a catalyst on Eisenhower and forced him to finalise an idea that had been shaping up in his mind all throughout the previous week: to dispense with the long proposed final thrust to Berlin (which would be carried out by Montgomery) and give Bradley the leading role in the last battle.

Although the precise details are still not clear, it is known that when in March Eisenhower began to confer with Bradley about the future conduct of the war, their common dislike of Montgomery and Bradley's desire completely to rehabilitate his reputation, slurred in the Ardennes, did to a certain extent act as a basis of their discussions. Naturally none of the participants have been eager to reveal how much personal considerations affected their thinking that month, but if we are to believe Ingersoll, who was present at Bradley's HQ during that period of time, 'Eisenhower stated flatly that he had several times given Montgomery more than enough to insure a victory and that, in each instance, Montgomery had failed him. The Supreme Commander didn't stop with Montgomery. At long last he vented his feelings about Churchill and attacked Churchill for his direct dealings with Montgomery, 'his meddlesomeness and his continued

Left: Churchill and Montgomery; the latter was Bradley's biggest problem *Above left:* Ernest Kaltenbrunner; supposed organiser of the mythical Alpine Redoubt. *Above right:* General George C Marshall

interference outside of channels'. In a cable, which, according to Ingersoll, was sent to Marshall at this time, Eisenhower said that he was concerned about the verdict of history and wondered whether the right people would get the credit for the Allied victories in the field. He then plunged into extravagant praise of Omar Bradley, stating that in his opinion Bradley had the finest mind for strategy of any of the Allied leaders. This was 'startling' because the emphasis was so thoroughly new for Eisenhower.

It was under these circumstances (if we are to believe Ingersoll) that 'Bradley made his historic decision – perhaps his only really history-making decision. Until that moment, while he had won battles and even whole campaigns, Bradley had operated on a single strategic decision (to destroy the German Army) made by others and simply handed to him. In deciding, after the Ruhr, to join with the Russians on the upper Elbe rather than to drive for Berlin, Bradley made a decision, absolutely on his own, which the British at least believe was an historic decision, which may yet leave its permanent mark on Europe'.

(Written immediately after the war and published in 1946 in Ingersoll's *Top Secret.*)

According to Ingersoll, Bradley who 'was complete master of the situation again', felt Berlin's capture would be an empty victory. For him the centre of German military power was now in the south and by driving north-east from Frankfurt to Berlin he would force more German troops into the supposed 'Alpine Redoubt'. If instead he were to drive due east and split Germany in two like 'Sherman through Georgia' with the US First and Ninth Armies, he would have the Third free for a juncture with the Russians in Czechoslovakia. And 'Bradley was so completely the boss that Eisenhower had no choice but to approve – and forwarding Bradley's plan he got approval back from Washington' (Ingersoll.)

In the end 'with all these things in mind it is a little less than fair to say that when Bradley submitted his plan to cut Germany in two, rather than race the Russians for Berlin, Eisenhower's approval was in any way forced. Bradley's plan gave him the opportunity to complete his gesture of self-assertion vis-a-vis the British

The Allied drive to the Elbe

Above: US infantrymen move up to secure the west bank of the Elbe. *Right:* Allied armour also on the move to secure the US bridgehead across the Elbe

and he promptly – and quite within his rights as the Supreme Commander – labelled the plan his own when he asked Washington's approval of it. And Washington did approve and the record in the Pentagon must certainly refer to the plan as the Supreme Commander's – which I am sure suited Omar Bradley, for the fireworks it touched off were not the kind he felt at home handling.'

Naturally we can not take Ingersoll's word alone for the source of the new plan, yet I think it is highly significant that after Eisenhower had conferred with Bradley that March, 12th Army Group HQ issued on 21st March, seven days before Eisenhower sent off his three telegrams, its 'Re-orientation of Strategy'.

This staff study pointed out that Eisenhower had received no directive from the Combined Chiefs of Staff about his military or political objectives save the vague instruction to attack 'the heart of Germany'. It was therefore up to him to define what was meant by the 'heart'. In Bradley's staff's opinion, Berlin was not that life-giving organ. According to the 'Re-orientation', new findings by intelligence had made the old strategy of the major thrust to Berlin obsolete: 'As reported by G-2 . . . all indications suggest that the enemy's political and military directorate is already in process of displacing to the "Redoubt" in Lower Bavaria'. It concluded with an implied criticism of Montgomery's strategic thinking, stating that 'localized centers of diminishing industrial or political significance weren't as important as large areas of territory. The metropolitan areas (i.e.Berlin) can no longer occupy a position of importance'.

The staff study now suggested that instead of allowing Montgomery to make a thrust to the north, Bradley's

Army Group should split Germany in two by driving through the centre. This would 'prevent German forces from withdrawing' towards the south and 'into the Redoubt'. This strategy would drive the enemy 'northwards where they can be rounded up against the shores of the Baltic and North Seas'.

General Bradley's only post-war comment on the subject has been: 'this obsession with the Redoubt . . . accounted for my gloomy caution on the probable end of the war in Europe'. And: 'Had Eisenhower even contemplated sending Montgomery ahead to Berlin, he would have had to reinforce that British Army with not less than one American Army [As it was Montgomery had to 'borrow' Ridgway's XVIII Airborne Corps in order to have sufficient strength to cross the Elbe]. I could see no political advantage accruing from the capture of Berlin that would offset the need for quick

destruction of the German Army on our front. As soldiers we looked naively on the British inclination to complicate the war with political foresight and non-military objectives'.

This statement aroused that doyen of military historians.General Fuller, to comment: 'If at the eleventh hour of a war political considerations are less important than military factors, well may it be asked, when are they more important'?

Thus it is that one might be tempted to draw the conclusion that the fatal Elbe decision was not based on strategic factors (and as we have seen from Bradley's words very definitely not political ones) but on personal factors. With Marshall in control in Washington (Admiral Leahy of the Joint Chiefs of Staff has gone on record as saying the Elbe decision was never discussed by the Joint Chiefs), Eisenhower had at last freedom to act as he wished without being

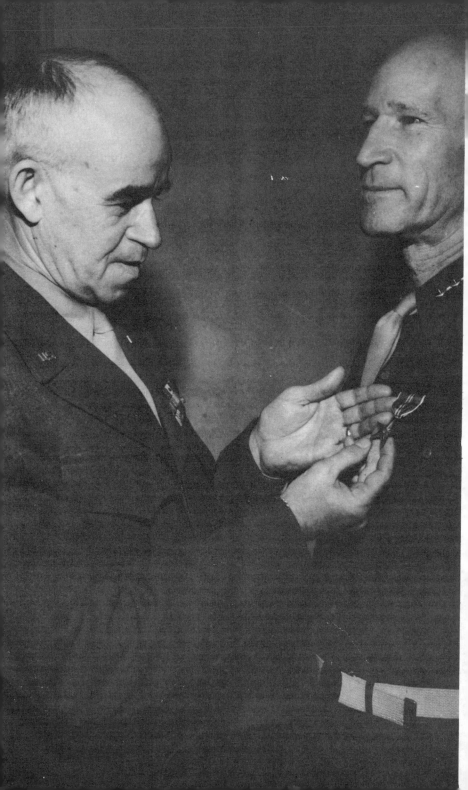

Left: Bradley decorates Lieutenant-General Simpson. *Above:* Montgomery, Churchill and Simpson; at this time there was considerable animosity between the Allies

bothered by any effective interference from Churchill, whose appeal to revoke the decision to the dying Roosevelt was fruitless. Just at that particular time in the history of the campaign, Montgomery's record as an aggressive commander was virtually nil and, in addition, he was proving himself particularly troublesome with his demands for absolute control of the ground forces and the single thrust to the north. Also at that same time, Bradley had completed his successful almost impromptu campaigns in the Rhineland and shown himself an aggressive leader, and very decidedly one who would not take lightly any further concessions to Montgomery. Had he not already threatened to resign and with him his most aggressive army commander Patton?

We cannot know what personal consideration must have gone through Eisenhower's mind at that particular time. Had he already begun to think of a political career after the war was over? He must have known that successful generals had always been offered political office in American history, going back through Pershing after the First World War (he had refused it) to Grant after the Civil War to the Founding Father himself, Washington. Already in March 1945 Patton had remarked that Eisenhower's actions were being governed by the fact that one day he would become President of the United States. Ingersoll, writing a little later, makes the same point. If this were the case (and one must remember that Eisenhower had been moving in top political circles for two years now, mixing freely with premiers, presidents and kings), then he must have realised that the future ex-GI voters and the Great American Public would not be too happy with a candidate who had

Next stop Berlin?

allowed a foreigner the triumph of the
final victory. If, however, General
Bradley and his men had the just credit
for the great triumph, the situation
would be changed greatly and in his
potential, political favour. As Ingersoll put it, SHAEF was beginning to
realise that the 'victory parades in
New York and Washington' were only
a few months away.

Bradley, still smarting from the
Ardennes and full of dislike for his
British rival, must have made Eisenhower fully aware of his own attitude
and the importance of the central
thrust for his own personal as well as

national prestige. As Ladislas Farago,
Patton's official biographer, has
summed it up: 'The plan represented
a belated victory for Bradley and
Patton. It gave them at last the main
thrust, a privilege and power they
had sought for so long without avail.'
But at this late stage, it was a hollow
victory and, in fact, not to the advantage of the cause of the Western Allies.

Sir Alan Brooke, Chief of the British
Imperial General Staff and Eisenhower's severest critic throughout
the campaign, also saw the change in
plan for what it was. Writing in his
diary on 1st April he remarks with
almost stoic resignation, for Brooke
realised the full political implications

of the Elbe decision: 'Most of the changes are due to national aspirations and to ensure that the US effort will not be lost under British command. It is all a pity and straightforward strategy is being affected by the nationalistic outlook of allies. This is one of the handicaps of operating with allies. But, as Winston says: "there is only one thing worse than fighting with allies, and that it fighting without them".'

Now, with six weeks of the war to go, Bradley had finally gained his head. In almost two years of campaigning, he had always been at some one else's command – Patton, Montgomery and then Eisenhower – men whose aid, perhaps, he had needed but who had consistently refused to let him go it his way. Now with effect from 28th March, the unassuming, somewhat retiring, gentle 'GI's General' (as the Press was beginning to call him in order to give him an image that might compete with that of 'Ike', 'Monty' and 'Old Blood an' Guts'), was going to run things his way in the brief period left to him before he passed into obscurity. Such is almost invariably the fate of the victorious soldier once the danger and the war are passed.

The last battles

On 1st April 1945 General Bradley controlled a massive force of over forty divisions, which, running from north to south, included Simpson's Ninth Army (officially returned to him from Montgomery's command on the 4th), Hodges' First, and Patton's Third. On that day, receiving Eisenhower's order that he was 'to mop up the Ruhr . . . launch a thrust with its main axis: Kassel-Leipzig . . . seize any opportunity to capture a bridgehead over the River Elbe and be prepared to conduct operations beyond the Elbe,' Bradley hurriedly finalised his plans for his Army Group. On 4th April he issued his own 'Letter of Instructions, No 20'. This instruction directed the Ninth to drive first for a line roughly south of Hanover, with the army centre in the approximate area of the little town of Hildesheim – roughly seventy miles from the River Elbe. Thereafter the second phase of the operation would begin. This second phase seemed to be in direct opposition to what Bradley and Eisenhower had decided in the last week of March. The key paragraph read: 'Phase 2. Advance on order to the east . . . exploit any opportunity for seizing a bridgehead over the Elbe and be prepared to continue

the advance on BERLIN or to the north-east'. One wonders why this direction was given, in view of Bradley's energetic rejection of Berlin. Was it just a subterfuge? Or did Bradley feel that if the Ninth did make a decisive breakthrough and was in a position to seize Berlin, it should do so. The prize would then be won by an American formation under his command and not by Montgomery as in the original plan.

We do not know. However, General Simpson jumped at the chance. 'My people were keyed up,' he recalled later. 'We'd been the first to the Rhine and now we were going to be the first to Berlin. All along we thought of just one thing – capturing Berlin, going through and meeting the Russians on the other side'. Immediately he received Bradley's Letter of Instructions, Simpson called his staff together and told the assembled officers 'to get an armored and an infantry division set up on the autobahn running just above Madgeburg on the Elbe to Potsdam, where we'll be ready to close in on Berlin'. Then it was the big, completely bald officer's intention to throw in the whole of his army, 'as fast as we can . . . if we get the bridgehead and they turn us loose'. As he told his staff: 'Damn, I want to get to Berlin and all you people, right down to the last private, I think, want it too.'

Meanwhile, to his rear, Field-Marshal Model's entrapped army in the Ruhr was preparing to make an attempt to break out at the industrial town of Hamm,as it was also to attempt to do at the town of Siegen on the First Army sector of the encircled Ruhr. But the attempt failed as it did at Siegen. A few days later the pocket was split and eventually in the third week of April, General Bradley's 12th Army Group took the surrender of more prisoners than had surrendered at Stalingrad or in Tunisia: some

Bradley with Assistant Secretary of War McCloy behind the lines

320,000 men and thirty generals at a cost of some 10,000 dead and wounded in the First and Ninth Armies.

But 'Big Simp', as he was called by his men, was not concerned with the Ruhr. His eyes were on Berlin; and Major-General Isaac White's over-sized 2nd Armored Division which was barrelling its way up the autobahn also had its sights set on being the first division to the Elbe and from thence the first in Berlin. Now on the Ninth Army's fifty odd miles of front, White's 'Hell on Wheels' division was spearheading the drive. Being with the 3rd, its rival in Hodges' First Army, one of the two remaining old, unreorganised armoured divisions, it had a tremendous number of vehicles which formed a stream seventy-two miles long. But White kept it moving with his harsh tongue and electric energy. (Even so, the division moving in tandem and averaging two miles per hour, took an average of twelve hours to pass a given point.)

The opposition was completely unpredictable. Some places were taken without a shot, the local burgomaster coming out to surrender his village or town before the first shot had been fired. Others were centres of desperate, fanatical resistance. In the Westphalian town of Detmold for instance, the 2nd Division simply drove through the town, with hardly a shot being fired. Yet a few hours later the follow-up infantry bumped into a group of SS soldiers who had moved into the town in the meantime and were forced to fight a bitter and prolonged battle to recapture it.

At Hamelin of Pied Piper fame, another SS unit tried to hold up the 2nd Armored in a similar manner. The follow-up infantry of the 3oth Infantry Division retaliated with heavy shelling until the town was reduced to rubble and occasioned Colonel Johnson of the Division's 117th Infantry Regiment to make the memorable statement: "This time we

got the rats out with a slightly different kind of flute'.

But nothing seemed able to stop the Ninth Army and its lead division, the 2nd. By the 10th, it had two corps pushing vigorously eastward against 'little or no resistance', with spearheads only a few miles short of Brunswick. Next day the drive accelerated and the 2nd Division made its final dash for the Elbe, in the firm belief that now it had passed Phase Line One – Hildesheim – it had the green light to cross the Elbe and proceed to Berlin.

In five huge columns, General White's division sped to the Elbe. They brushed aside everything in their way. On one occasion a major in the 2nd lined his thirty-four tanks up as if they were cavalry and gave the order 'Charge!' Guns blazing, the Shermans rushed a German position and the enemy fled. By Wednesday evening 11th April, in an unparalleled armored thrust, the 2nd's tanks had driven fifty-seven miles (and 226 miles altogether since the division had crossed the Rhine nineteen days earlier) in just under twenty-four hours. It was a tremendous performance but also indicative of just how weak the Germans were and, incidentally, a criticism of Bradley's statement on the 100,000 casualties Berlin might cost him. Shortly after 2000 hours that evening Colonel Disney of the lead armored regiment sent his headquarters the laconic message: 'We're on the Elbe.'

In fact, one small group of armored vehicles, travelling at 55mph in some cases, had managed to breach the western suburbs of Magdeburg. The armored cars were forced back, but did report that the bridge across the river which carried the autobahn eastwards was still intact. Immediately White switched his attack to the bridge, but was driven off by heavy artillery fire. It was clear that he was not going to be able to take the bridge on the run. Meanwhile another group of the Division's 67th Armored Regiment was attempting a surprise attack on another bridge across the Elbe at the small town of Schönebeck. Under the command of a Major Hollingsworth who was a dead shot and wore his 45s strapped low on his hips western style, the little group came on the bridge just as the light started to fail. Hollingsworth did not hesitate. Hatches buttoned up, his Shermans charged the bridge at the rear of a group of German tanks attempting to escape to the other side. A German Mark V tried to hold the Americans up, but Hollingsworth's own tank opened up first and put the German out of action. The column roared on through a scene of chaos in which, as Hollingsworth was to put it later, 'everyone was firing at everyone else. It was the damnedest mess. Germans were hanging out of windows, either shooting at us with their Panzerfausts or just dangling in death'. Although his tank was hit and he himself wounded Hollingsworth got to the Schönebeck bridge. He was forced back. But another group attempted to take it at dawn, but they were too late. At that time on 12th April the Germans blew the bridge up in their faces.

Denied bridges and still believing that the Ninth was going on to Berlin, the 2nd Armored decided to go ahead without a bridge. On mid-afternoon 12th April Simpson came to the conclusion that the only solution was an amphibious assault in order to secure a bridgehead on the Elbe's eastern shore. Thereafter he would have a pontoon bridge built. The task was given to Brigadier-General Hinds, CO of the 2nd's Combat Command B.

He decided to make his assault at Westerhüsen, south of Magdeburg. He knew the risk he was taking, especially if the enemy managed to bring up artillery. But he took a chance. At 2000 hours two battalions of armored infantry were quietly ferried to the opposite bank. The crossing was

German prisoners captured by the Allies

US forces in the north push on
through the ruins of Germany

unopposed. By midnight, the two battalions were completely over and by dawn another battalion had joined them. Quickly they deployed and began to dig in while at divisional headquarters a jubilant General White called General Simpson and told him 'We're across'!

Meanwhile the US First Army had been making rapid progress, though it was further from the Elbe than the Ninth and it was taking higher casualties because its sector of the front contained two areas of fairly strong resistance. In the Harz mountains there were 70,000 surviving members of the German Eleventh Army, which although lacking heavy weapons, had an ideal site for resistance based on infantry and infantry weapons. Further on there were such towns as Dessau, Halle and Leipzig, which although badly battered, contained units prepared to defend them to the last.

Hodges, however, concentrated on a rapid advance. Leaving his infantry to contain and eradicate these stumbling blocks, his armor pushed on in

Above: Montgomery's troops in the north try to keep pace with Bradley in the south. *Right:* Supreme Allied Commander General Dwight D Eisenhower

the gaps and drove almost unopposed to the River Mulde, where the two corps on the right seized two bridges virtually unopposed on the 15th April

The chief town in the area, Leipzig still held out however. But already the road and rail network with south Germany was severed, which meant that the various German commands were cut off from each other. It was obvious to Hodges that little resistance could be expected anymore from the enemy. The Germans on his front were well and truly beaten. What now? It was the same question that some miles to the north General Simpson was asking himself too What now?

But the future of the two American armies had already been virtually decided the day before. On the 14th Eisenhower telegraphed the Combined Chiefs of Staff his future intentions:

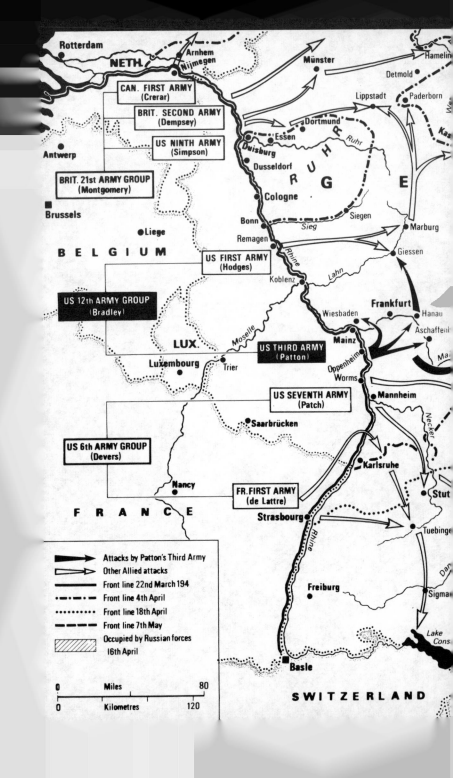

Rotterdam
NETH.
Arnhem
Nijmegen
Münster
Hamelin
Detmold
Paderborn
CAN. FIRST ARMY
(Crerar)
Lippstadt
BRIT. SECOND ARMY
(Dempsey)
Dortmund
Essen
Kas
Ruhr
US NINTH ARMY
(Simpson)
Duisburg
R U H R
Dusseldorf
Antwerp
E
BRIT. 21st ARMY GROUP
(Montgomery)
Cologne
G
Brussels
Bonn
Siegen
Liege
Marburg
Remagen
Sieg
BELGIUM
Rhine
Giessen
US FIRST ARMY
(Hodges)
Koblenz
Lahn
US 12th ARMY GROUP
(Bradley)
Frankfurt
Wiesbaden
Hanau
LUX.
Moselle
Aschaffenb
Luxembourg
Trier
US THIRD ARMY
(Patton)
Mainz
Ma
Oppenheim
Worms
US SEVENTH ARMY
(Patch)
Mannheim
Saarbrücken
Neckar
US 6th ARMY GROUP
(Devers)
Karlsruhe
Nancy
FR. FIRST ARMY
(de Lattre)
Stut
F R A N C E
Strasbourg
Tuebinge
Rhine
Freiburg
Dan
Sigma

Attacks by Patton's Third Army
Other Allied attacks
Front line 22nd March 194
Front line 4th April
Front line 18th April
Front line 7th May
Occupied by Russian forces
16th April

Lake
Cons

0   Miles   80
0   Kilometres   120

Basle
SWITZERLAND

Lieutenant-General Courtney H Hodges.

'A. In the central area to hold a firm front on the Elbe. B. To undertake operations to the Baltic at Lübeck and to Denmark (Montgomery). C. To make a powerful thrust in the Danube valley to join with the Russians and break up the southern redoubt. D. As the thrust on Berlin must await the success of these three operations I do not include it as a part of my present plan. The essence of my plan is to stop on the Elbe and clean up my flanks'. To emphasise his decision to stop on the Elbe, he telegraphed Marshall the next day to state that not only were the Baltic and Bavarian objectives more important than Berlin, but that to plan for an immediate effort to Berlin 'would be foolish in view of the relative situation of the Russians and ourselves . . . While it is true that only our spearheads are up to that river; our center of gravity is well back of there'. It was left to General Bradley who, if we are to believe some sources was the originator of the stop-on-the-Elbe decision, to break the news to General Simpson, whose army was in the best position for the attack on Berlin from the west.

Early on Sunday morning 15th April, Simpson received a call from Bradley. The former was to fly immediately to 12th Army Group HQ at Wiesbaden. 'I've something very im portant to tell you,' Bradley said 'and I don't want to say it on th phone'.

Bradley was waiting for Simpso at the airfield. 'We shook hands, Simpson recalled later, 'and there an then he told me the news. Brad said 'You must stop on the Elbe. You ar not to advance any farther in th direction of Berlin. I'm sorry, Simp but there it is'.

'Where in the hell did you get this' Simpson demanded.

'From Ike'.

Simpson was so stunned that h could not 'even remember half of th things Brad said from then on. All remember is that I was so heartbroke and I got back on the plane in a kin of a daze. All I could think of was How am I going to tell my staff, m corps commanders and my troops Above all, how am I going to tell m troops'?

From his HQ Simpson passed th news to his corps commanders, the he went to the bridgehead on the Rive Elbe commanded by General Hinds Hinds saw the commander's worrie look and thought that 'maybe the ol man didn't like the way we wer crossing the river. He asked how I wa getting along'. Hinds answered: ' guess we're all right now, General We had two good withdrawals. Ther was no excitement and no panic an our Barby crossings are going good'.

'Fine,' Simpson replied. 'Keep som of your men on the east bank if yo want to. But they're not to go an farther'. He continued. 'Sid, this is a far as we're going.' Hinds was shocke into insubordination. 'No, sir,' he said 'That's not right. We're going t Berlin'.

According to Hinds, Simpson seeme to struggle with his emotions. Ther was a moment of uneasy silence. The Simpson said in a voice that wa without emotion: 'We're not going t Berlin, Sid. This is the end of the wa for us'.

The following day Simpson an

Hodges got their orders. They were to defend the Elbe-Mulde line and hold the existing Elbe bridgehead, 'as a threat to Berlin' unless driven back by a superior enemy force. The Third Army, commanded by Patton, on the other hand, was to launch a 'powerful attack to gain contact with the Soviet forces in the Danube valley and seize Salzburg'.

Now, while the two northern armies of General Bradley's Army Group were left to sit out the war, the remaining fighting was left to General Patton. As right at the beginning, the fates of the two men were to be inextricatibly linked right to the end.

Towards the end of the First and Ninth's advance to the Elbe and Mulde, Patton had marked time and regrouped preparatory to his attack towards the Danube. His forces built up by First Army divisions released by the surrender of Model in the Ruhr, he now prepared to side-slip southwards and join up with General Patch's Seventh Army for the attack, which was to be the combined effort of the two armies (understandably General Patch wasn't too eager to work with Patton, knowing the latter's talent for gaining the laurels of any battle he was engaged in for himself, but the Seventh Army Commander had no other choice).

On 20th April, the Third Army, Bradley's last active command, started to move southward. Two days later it jumped off. It met little opposition, save at Neumarkt and Regensburg and along the line of the Altmuhl, Danube and Isar rivers. Swiftly it thrust through Bavaria and swept into Austria, led by a massive three corps attack. Within a matter of hours the threat of the Alpine Redoubt, defended by powerful fanatical last-ditch Nazi troops, was shown to be what it was: a composition of clever propaganda, Swiss fears and newspapermen's copy.

With the Alpine Redoubt proved a meaningless legend, Czechoslovakia loomed up large in Patton's plans –

and in those of the British Government. On the 30th Churchill put it to the American president: 'There can be little doubt,' he told Truman, 'that the liberation of Prague and as much as possible of the territory of western Czechoslovakia by your forces might make the whole difference to the post-war situation in Czechoslovakia and might well influence that in nearby countries . . . Of course,' he added, 'such a move by Eisenhower must not interfere with his main operations against the Germans, but I think the highly important consideration mentioned above should be brought to his attention'.

But Marshall was again against fighting for political objectives. He told Eisenhower on the 28th: 'Personally and aside from all logistic, tactical or strategical implications I should be loath to hazard American lives for purely political purposes'.

Eisenhower replied that he already had other priorities and besides in his opinion the Red Army would reach Czechoslovakia first and enter the capital before the Americans. He assured General Marshall: 'I shall not attempt any move I deem militarily unwise to gain a political prize unless I receive specific orders from the Combined Chiefs of Staff'. For Eisenhower the main consideration seemed to be to ensure that his forces advancing from the west did not accidentally clash with the Russians coming from the east. Thus it was that Eisenhower forced Bradley to halt Patton while he waited to hear from the Russians about their intentions in Czechoslovakia. For four days the Americans waited, save for a few minor skirmishes, while the Russian troops earmarked to take Prague were still busy inside Germany at Dresden and Görlitz.

Then at 1930 hours on 4th May, Bradley called Patton at the latter's CP. 'Ike has just called,' he said excitedly. 'You have the green light for Czechoslovakia, George. When can you move'?

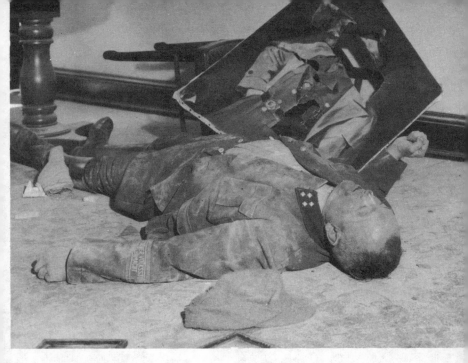

Left: Germany mobilises youngsters to defend the fatherland. *Above:* Some, like the General of Volksstrum at Leipzig, did not surrender

'Tomorrow morning,' Patton replied without hesitation.

Bradley was a little sceptical but not as sceptical as he had been in the old days in France. 'As we were pretty well used to each other,' Patton wrote later, 'he believed me'.

But Patton's eagerness to attack into the new country puzzled Bradley. 'Why does everyone in the Third Army want to liberate the Czechs'? In a high good mood, Patton replied: 'Oh Brad, can't you see? The Czechs are our *allies* and consequently their women aren't off limits. [At this time there were still penalties for soldiers of the Allied armies found fraternising with Germans of both sexes.] On to Czechoslovakia and fraternization!' he yelled into the telephone. 'How in hell can you stop an army with a battle cry like that!'

Between 0800 and 1000 hours on 5th May, Patton's XII jumped off, its 5th and 90th Infantry Divisions crossing into Czechoslovakia itself, while the 11th Armored and the 26th Infantry Divisions headed for Linz, which they took the same day. Meanwhile a little later the new V Corps joined in the attack.

But Patton was restricted in his movements. Bearing in mind Eisenhower's strict instructions about stop lines, Bradley told Patton he must restrict his advance to a northwest-southeast line running through Pilsen. But in his usual manner he allowed Patton more freedom than Eisenhower had intended. He suggested that Patton 'could and should reconnoiter vigorously as far as Prague'. For the man who had captured Palermo in Sicily two years before in an operation which had been labelled a 'reconnaissance in force' and had pretty liberally used his 'rock soup method' of getting himself involved in action ever since, Patton took this to mean he had Bradley's permission to take Prague.

By late afternoon on the fifth day of May, with the war only a couple of days to go before it ended, Patton

pressed home his attack in Czechoslovakia. His 1st Division drove on Karlsbad while his 97th Infantry headed for Pilsen, the troops spurred on by the knowledge that the town was the world's most famous beer-producing town. Meanwhile elements of his lightly armored cavalry groups were speeding towards Klatovy and Prasily. At the same time the 90th Infantry Division opened up the road through the Regen Pass so that Patton's armor could debouch into the plains beyond. And Patton's most famous division, the 4th Armored, which had been at the head of his advance ever since he let the division loose in Brittany (and had gone through three divisional commanders, incidentally, in the process), was reconnoitering routes to Prague, which it intended to attack on a large scale the following morning.

But an American OSS team had beaten Hoge's Fourth to Prague. A jeep team led by Captain Eugene Fodor, a Slovak-American, had penetrated the Czech capital and made contact with General Frantisek Kratochwil, head of the partisans, who held the capital, and who surrendered the city to the young American captain. Hastily Fodor retraced his steps till he reached Major General Huebner, who commanded Patton's V Corps. The latter acted at once.

He arranged for a combat command of the 9th Armored to get ready to seize Prague, but his decision worried General Patton. His orders stipulated he should stop on the Pilsen line – and Prague was at least sixty miles to the northeast. What should he do?

He decided to call Bradley. He told him his situation and then asked: 'Is this stop line through Pilsen really mandatory? Can't you let me go into Prague? For God's sake, Brad, those patriots in the city need our help! We

Above Left: British gunners using US 155mm guns (Long Toms) shell the east bank of the Elbe. *Left:* Russian and American troops meet on the Elbe

Field-Marshal Keitel, Chief of the German Combined Staff, signs the unconditional surrender document

have no time to lose!'

Bradley said he understood, but he would have to find out what Eisenhower's attitude was. At this stage of the campaign when everything was going his way, General Bradley did not want to chance a break with the Supreme Commander. He said he would call Eisenhower at once. But then Patton had one of his brainstorms. He had done it before and it had worked. Why not now? He would 'get lost' on the following day, 6th May, and while he was lost, his soldiers would enter Prague. Once in the capital, he would 'be found' and report to Bradley from a telephone box in Prague's main square.

Bradley refused to commit himself. He wanted to see what Eisenhower thought first. But the Supreme Commander, anxious to avoid any clash with the Russians, militarily or politically, vetoed Patton's plan. The political reward of the capture of Prague did not interest him; he was concerned solely with military values. Already the day before he had been in touch with General Alexei Antonov, the Red Army's chief of staff, who urged him not 'to move the Allied forces in Czechoslovakia east of the originally intended line' to avoid, as Antonov put it, 'a possible confusion of forces'.

As Eisenhower had agreed to Antonov's wishes, he now emphasised to Bradley to tell Patton wherever he was that in no circumstances was he to go in force beyond the Budweis-Karlsbad-Pilsen line. Prague was not to be touched.

Bradley called Patton on the following morning. He told Patton what Eisenhower had ordered. 'The halt line through Pilsen is mandatory for V and XII Corps, George,' he emphasised. 'Moreover you must not, I repeat not, reconnoiter to a greater depth than five miles north-east of Pilsen. Ike does not want any international complications at this late date'.

'For God's sake, Brad,' Patton protested. 'It seems to me that a great nation like America should let others worry about complications'.

As US official historian summed it up later: 'By this action [Eisenhower] left Prague and most of Czechoslovakia to be liberated by the Red Forces. Except for minor adjustments of boundaries and the closing up to lines of demarcation, operations of the Western Allies were at an end'.

On that same day General Bradley went to bed shortly after midnight. But he didn't sleep for long. At 0400 the next morning, the phone rang. It was the Supreme Commander calling from Reims.

'Brad,' he said, 'it's all over'.

The Germans had surrendered.

Bradley was awake now. He called Patton first, an indication of how much he thought of the Third Army commander in relation to his other army commanders. 'Ike just called me, George,' he told Patton. 'The Germans have surrendered. It takes effect at midnight 8th May. We're to hold in place everywhere up and down the line. There's no sense in taking any more casualties now'.

He then called Hodges, Simpson and finally Gerow, who commanded the newly-formed Fifteenth Army, intended for occupation duties. Repeating the message, he waited till they had digested the news and then got dressed. It was 0630 and he could hear the rattle of the soldiers' mess tins outside as they lined up for food.

Finally he put on his helmet, for there were still twenty-four hours till the end of combat operations was officially approved. On its front glittered the four silver stars of a four star general. Now the man who five years before had been in civilian clothes, but now commanded forty-three divisions stretched out over the 640 mile front of the 12th Army Group, walked over the room to the mapboard and wrote in the new date: D plus 335.

The greatest year in General Omar Nelson Bradley's life was over.

Bradley and Marshal Koniev

Bradley after the war

General Bradley did not stay very long in Europe after the war was over. Eisenhower did not need him for occupation duties as he did his most famous subordinate commander Patton. He was scheduled to go to the Pacific Theatre, but the war in the Far East ended before he could be used there. Instead on 15th August 1945, he was appointed Administrator of Veterans Affairs, an unthankful post. But Bradley stuck it for two years, ensuring that millions of men who had served under him and other commanders in Europe and the Far East had a good start in civilian life, concerning himself with such mundane matters (after the high excitement of the war) as the GI Bill, Veteran Housing, Loans etc.

On 1st December 1947 he relinquished the post to familiarise himself once again with Army problems before taking on his new duties as Chief of Staff on 7th February 1948, succeeding his former boss in the post – Dwight D Eisenhower. A year later on 16th August 1949, he was sworn in as the first Chairman of the Joint Chiefs of Staff and on 16th August, 1951 was reappointed for a further two-year term, carrying out the tasks of Chairman at a particularly difficult period of American history, during the Korean War. But he survived the onerous duties well and on 20th September, 1950 he was made General of the Army, which granted him the honour of being America's fourth five-star Army general officer: the only one from the war to survive till this day.

At the first meeting of the 12 Atlantic Pact nations in Washington in 1949. General Bradley was appointed the first Chairman of Military Committee of the North Atlantic Treaty Organisation. At the termination of his term of office, he continued until August 1953 as United States Representative to the Military Committee of NATO and in doing so exercised great responsibi-

The great rivals; Patton, Bradley and Montgomery

lity in the co-ordination of the military efforts of the free world. Thereafter General Bradley slowly disappeared from the military scene, appearing occasionally to advise presidents or to take part in official memorial ceremonies, outliving many of the men whom he had served under, such as Eisenhower and Marshall, and many of those who had served under him, Patton and Hodges, for instance.

Yet although General Bradley is still alive twenty-five years after the conclusion of the Second World War and there has been a mass of material published about him and those close to him, he is still an unknown quantity. Eisenhower, Montgomery, Patton etc – they have all had private and professional chroniclers, the Codmans, Faragos, Wilmots, Mooreheads, Butchers, Summersbys etc – who have dissected both their private and professional lives during those fateful months of 1944-1945. But apart from General Bradley's own memoir *A Soldier's Story* (written six years after the war and to which the General sticks without deviation till this very day) and the very subjective Ingersoll book *Top Secret*, we have had very little published material in the quarter of a century which has passed since the war ended that tells very much more about Omar Bradley than was already known in June 1944 when he first saw France from the deck of the *USS Augusta*.

The general impression still remains of a relatively gentle and retiring man, who was content to obey Eisenhower's and, to a certain extent, Montgomery's dictates for most of the campaign until, after the Ardennes, when his anger was finally roused, he began to force the Supreme Commander's hand and fight for an independent role. Yet even then he could not completely break the hold his one-time superior Patton had over him still and was forced to accept some of the more outrageous actions to which the hot-headed Third Army commander was addicted, such as Patton's

decision to raid Hammelburg POW camp with no authority from Bradley, a raid carried out at some loss for completely personal reasons. This seems to be the general picture even at late as 1970 when we know a lot more about the intrigues and personal aspirations of the senior commanders concerned in the 1944-1945 campaign than we did in 1945.

Nor has Bradley inspired a military writer or historian, such as Martin Blumenson who took up Patton's campaign or Forrest Pogue who championed certain of Eisenhower's more controversial actions or the Britisher RW Thompson with his hate-love relationship for Montgomery, to reappraise his conduct of military actions. As yet no one has tried to estimate what exactly was Bradley's special contribution to the campaign: his unique part in those operations which ended the war and incidentally helped to change the face of Europe for better or for worse.

Let us then attempt first of all to make an assessment of the philosophy and psychology of this general whom I have characterised at the beginning of his campaign in Europe as being a 'military *tabula rasa* '. What kind of man was General Omar Nelson Bradley?

For the 'Great American Public' at least, General Bradley was discovered by Ernie Pyle, the great American war reporter. In 1943, in Africa, Eisenhower told the undersized reporter, who was killed himself in action two years later: 'Next time you're up front, go and discover Bradley'. As a result Pyle went and interviewed the new commander. In a series of six columns, he introduced the plain, unassuming general to the public, and started the newspaper and later radio stories which stamped Bradley as the 'GIs' General'. By this was meant that he was the most democratic and unassuming commander in the American Army, who was accessible to everyone and avoided like the plague the trappings that went with high command. After the war, to support this thesis, attention was drawn to Bradley's own implied criticism of Patton's high-handed and autocratic way of life when the former wrote in his memoirs that the GIs were not impressed by Patton's gleaming staff officers and open touring cars with the oversized general's stars attached to their sides. And indeed, as Bradley himself writes of the occasion when his aide Hansen suggested to him he should see Pyle: 'Thirty-two years in the peacetime army had taught me to do my job, hold my tongue and keep my name out of the papers'. But Hansen convinced him and 'For three days Ernie Pyle and I were inseparable. We breakfasted together in the morning on powdered eggs and soyabean cereal. After the staff briefing we hung dust goggles round our necks and headed off to see the divisions. Lunches we ate on the road – tinned cheese from the K-ration and a sticky fruit bar for dessert. And in the evenings we cut the dust in our throats with a jigger of Oliver Leese's Scotch'.

On the fourth day Pyle returned again to his beat with the GIs.' My friends will accuse me of having sold out to the brass,' he explained with a sad smile.

Thus we have the retiring newly appointed general exposed for the very first time to the publicity machine which was going to be a permanent feature of high command ever afterwards, and obviously liking it, for doesn't the emphasis on the humble food suggest that he soon learned the lesson the publicity men had taught him and was living up to his image as the 'GIs' general'? (Even such a noted ascetic as Montgomery did not believe in making himself uncomfortable during his campaigns, whereas many of Bradley's comrades like Eisenhower and Patton lived exceedingly well during the war.) Although Bradley did not establish his own press camp till after the Ardennes fiasco, after those three days with Pyle, he succumbed to the temptations of the press completely and in a very American way so that public opinion, formed by newspaper and radio, became increasingly important to him and his making of decisions right throughout the rest of the war.

When the GIs' general theme began to run thin in 1944, the newspapermen created a new image for Bradley, which made him not only the most democratic of American generals but also in many ways the brain behind the high command. Thus even at the time of the Sicilian campaign, the press reported the story that the GIs were saying: 'Patton conquered the island in thirty-eight days because he had a secret weapon – Bradley!' It was not surprising, therefore, that by March 1945 Ralph Ingersoll, a former newspaper editor himself and a lieutenant colonel on Bradley's staff, could maintain that Bradley was 'so completely the boss', with Churchill telephoning him personally and 'going over Eisenhower's head' asking him not to retreat from the Elbe because he wished to bargain with this territory for concessions from the Russians. (Ingersoll also states: 'At the time Bradley had been given to understand that he was to remain in Europe after the surrender, to command the American occupation. Whether it was in any way related to this conversation with the Prime Minister is not known, but Eisenhower relieved Bradley of responsibility for the occupation shortly thereafter and the latter's career as a general in the field was over'.)

But beneath the image created by the publicity machinery there seems to have been for most of the campaign a Bradley who was modest and retiring. He seemed to dislike paperwork and written orders and preferred to fly to his army commanders to give them their orders orally. As a result his staff officers weren't overworked, often being kept busy with staff studies rather than the high pressure work of the moment. In fact, one gets the impression of a lonely man, running his show by himself, unable to let his hair down to his senior staff officers. Always alert and

Bradley as Chairman of the Joint Chiefs of Staff, 1949

responsive, Bradley, however, never seemed deeply disturbed, and Ingersoll records that 'I never heard him say a harsh word to anyone'.

How does one explain this dislike of paperwork, the emphasis on oral orders (Chester Wilmot, the Australia historian of the campaign and occasional newspaperman at Bradley's HQ, notes this tendency too), and his lack of intimates among his senior staff? Ladislas Farago, Patton's biographer, sees Bradley as a man whose 'vistas were limited by a creeping timidity; although Bradley could clearly see his opportunities and had the intellectual resources to plan for them, an innate caution restrained him from going all the way'. Such a man would be hesitant to make a bold decision and then commit it to paper or discuss it with his staff; he would be more inclined to mull it over in his head and then 'bull it out' with his

army commanders so that whatever appeared might be taken as a joint decision and a joint responsibility Then if the decision did not work out as planned, there would be no definite written statement to be used against one.

And perhaps there is a certain amount of hesitancy in Bradley's decision-making throughout the early and middle stages of the campaign which could have been motivated by Bradley's 'innate caution' (as Farago terms it) and the fact that he was still somewhat unsure of himself. Then, in spite of both Eisenhower's and Patton's meteoric rises during the war, the former had been dealing with high ranking officers and politicians in Washington since 1929 and the latter was exceedingly wealthy and naturally imperious. Bradley, on the other hand, had had neither of these advantages and was to some degree awed and impressed by his meteoric career during the war. (The very last passage in his memoirs makes this point when the general writes: 'Only five years before on May 7, as a lieutenant-colonel in civilian clothes, I had ridden a bus down Connecticut Avenue to my desk in the old Munitions Building'.) To counteract this awe, he was somewhat forceful in his relations with his superiors, yet at the same time unsure of himself.

It is, therefore, not surprising that Bradley formed a special relationship with Patton and not with Hodges or Simpson. Simpson came too late upon the scene with his Ninth Army to come into consideration. Hodges, on the other hand, had been in Europe right from the start. After all,he had been Bradley's deputy while Bradley had commanded the First Army during the initial stages of Invasion. Yet in some ways, Hodges himself reflected Bradley's own uncertainties. It often seemed to him that his army took the brunt of the fighting yet received the smaller share of the praise which so often went to Patton. Hodges was a difficult and somewhat equivocal man; not the kind Bradley, with his own personal problem, could rely upon.

Patton was different. He was Bradley's former boss and used to giving orders to his now chief and he was naturally autocratic and outspoken with no time for equivocation. In addition, the employment of his army (so often relegated to a minor role) often coincided with Bradley's attempts to fight SHAEF. Patton, as a result, knew that to support Bradley meant that his own ends would be achieved, and vice-versa.

Thus the two men, so patently dissimilar, formed a special relationship throughout the campaign: a relationship which raises the question of how far Bradley's decisions were influenced by Patton. Naturally a man of Bradley's retiring middle-class temperament was appalled by a lot of what he saw of Patton. He never understood Patton's apparent indifference to logistics, for Bradley as well as Eisenhower and Montgomery were constantly concerned with logistics

throughout the campaign (at times one is tempted to think that it is their major concern). Nor could he ever tolerate Patton's vulgar public personality, with his weakness for profanity and often pathological hunger for public recognition and power. As Bradley remarked at the end of their first period of association in North Africa: 'However successful he [Patton] was as a corps commander, [he] had not yet learned to command himself.'

Naturally it is difficult to establish in the hurly-burly of war who first thought of what. All one can say is that Patton's plans and ideas were documented and written down prior to his death in December 1948 while Bradley's first appeared in his memoirs of 1951. The latter obviously could not be contested by Patton as the Third Army commander was by then dead. Yet there is some indication that in France and later in the Eifel Patton helped to make Bradley's mind up for him. For instance, when he and Bradley flew to Middleton's VIII Corps HQ at Morlaix on 31st August 1944 to discuss with the latter his siege of Brest, Bradley was decidely pessimistic about his chances of capturing the Breton sea port. Patton during the course of the discussions remarked slyly he was tired of fighting on four fronts at once. By this he hoped that Bradley would free him of the tiresome chore of taking Brest and let him get on with more important campaigning. The remark had its effect and Patton could write later: 'Bradley, as usual, had been thinking the same thing'. The 'as usual' was meant to be ironic.

And it is true that Patton's very partisan staff felt that Bradley was succeeding in France by plagiarizing Patton's ideas, deliberately or otherwise. As Lieutenant-Colonel Codman, Patton's aide and biographer, wrote to his wife at the time: 'As of August 1st ... General Bradley has adopted practically all of General Patton's plans'.

Whatever the truth of this matter is,

one thing is clear, Patton's special relationship with Bradley and his highly individualistic manner of conducting his operations, meant that Bradley gave undue priority to the Third Army throughout the campaign. (Patton often explained his tactic of getting himself involved in an armed reconnaissance which necessitated building up by additional troops until it became a full-scale battle by the analogy of two tramps preparing 'rock soup'. Starting off with two polished stones, they ask a housewife for a little water to boil them in, then for a few vegetables and a little later for a little seasoning. Finally they ask for and get meat. Now they have their 'rock soup'.) And so we come to a major result of General Bradley's uncertain frame of mind, a compound of all the factors which have been discussed so far: By virtue of his reliance on and predilection for General George Patton and his Third Army, General Bradley helped to drag the whole balance of Allied military

power out of shape, i.e. by pulling it from its originally northern bias, and thus changed the whole basis of Allied strategy.

Let us have a look at how this came about. As we have seen, right from the day his army was activated Patton was determined to fight the campaign his way. His drive for the Breton ports indicates that. Under normal circumstances either Eisenhower or Bradley would have soon brought him to heel. But Eisenhower, as most military historians must surely admit today, did not command his wide flung armies during the campaign; the task was simply too big for one man, whatever Field-Marshal Montgomery was to say to the contrary. As for Bradley, he needed Patton, indiscretions, impetuousness and all, because for him

Patton represented the only means of counteracting Montgomery's preponderance to the north. Patton was a worthy equal of Montgomery in ability and newsworthiness; and he stood head and shoulders above Hodges and Simpson, (it is interesting to conjecture what might have happened if Hodges instead of Patton had been in command of the Third Army.) As a result Bradley knew that Patton was his particular ace up the sleeve when it came to drawing attention away from Montgomery up in the north down to himself in the south.

Of course, at first the Montgomery-Bradley rivalry was an artificial thing, the product of some newspapermen's imaginations. But as the early months of the campaign passed and it became obvious that Montgomery was serious about trying to retain control of all the ground forces (He officially relinquished the overall command on 1st September 1944) and that, failing this

he wanted to ensure that the major thrust should be made in his sector with a sizeable portion of Bradley detached to him to enable him to do so so, Bradley began to take the Montgomery threat to his newly-won power seriously. In addition, he was growing in status and power, with his forty odd divisions clearly outnumbering the Britisher's fourteen. Consequently Patton's persistent claims that his Third Army should always play a major part in every campaign, even if this negatively affected Hodges and even if it damaged the whole overall strategy, coincided with Bradley's own desires.

In fact, as soon as Patton appeared on the scene, Bradley's relationships with both Montgomery and later Hodges (when he took over the First) began to deteriorate. This deterioration coincided with the end of the set-piece battle, of which Montgomery was the master, and the start of the

battles of exploitation. Now the new Army Group Commander trying to cope with Patton, was, as RW Thompson has put it: 'like a man clinging to the mane of a half wild stallion, dazzled and confused by the opportunities growing with every hour'. Almost immediately the two American generals started to criticise Montgomery, who was still nominally their boss until the end of August. Praising himself that month, Patton wrote: 'The 3rd Army had advanced farther and faster than any army in history... we never had to regroup, which seemed to be the chief form of amusement in the British armies'. Filled with contempt for 'the rabbit' – Montgomery's slowness. he urged Bradley half seriously to let him drive Montgomery back into the sea with one of his corps.

By the end of that month Bradley was becoming aware of Montgomery's determination to fight for the 'narrow thrust strategy' and although the former did not share Eisenhower's predilection for the 'broad front' approach, he was determined to support Eisenhower's strategy until he could convince the Supreme Commander that he, Bradley, should carry out the narrow thrust in his own sector.

So the months passed with nothing decided until the enemy settled the issue for the Allies by means of the surprise Ardennes counter-attack. As we have seen, the word 'surprise' should be qualified. The Battle of the Bulge did not come altogether as a surprise. Intelligence was aware that something was about to happen along Hodges' front. Strong had warned Bradley of the weaknesses of his Ardennes sector in the first week of December. Hodges, too, had reacted to the warnings of his own intelligence men by asking Bradley for two further divisions and had been turned down. (Though it must be admitted that Hodges didn't feel the enemy attack would come through the Ardennes, but probably near the Roer area.) In

fact, it is clear that Bradley did expect some form of enemy attack prior to 16th December when the German offensive started. His remarks to General Strong, 'Let them come', and to Bedell Smith on the afternoon of 16th December, when the news of attack was revealed to the replacement conference and Smith remarked 'You've been wishing for a counter-attack. Now it looks as though you've got it,' seem to confirm this.

But Bradley was obviously so preoccupied with Patton's planned attack in the Saar (after all he first thought the German counter-offensive was a 'spoiling attack to force à halt on Patton's advances into the Saar'), that he refused to consider any possibility which might force him to modify his plans. While Montgomery was halted in Holland, he wanted to ensure that Patton was involved in offensive operations and that the latter had sufficient resources to make his progress swift and eye-catching. For the first time since the start of the 1944-1945 campaign, Bradley felt that Eisenhower had taken away Montgomery's northern priority and given it to him in the south. As a result he was prepared to take a risk in the Ardennes – not as planned and carefully worked out as he indicated in his memoirs, but still a risk. He told Middleton, who commanded the VIII Corps guarding the long Ardennes front to 'simulate the movements of additional units into his area in order to draw enemy divisions to his front. He had carried out part of these activities early in the month [December] and was told to resume the program later'.

These last statements indicate how little Bradley realised what was the state of his Ardennes defenses and how completely pre-occupied he was with Patton's Saar offensive. The resultant German attack which caught him completely off his guard did not change his attitude to the southern push. If anything it strengthened his determination to draw the main

US forces serving in Korea were Bradley's responsibility

weight of the Allied attack from the north to the south. It is clear that during the months of February and March Bradley did little to restrain his army commanders, Hodges and Patton, from involving themselves in offensive operations that would inevitably affect the course of Montgomery's push in the north. When both Hodges and later Patton seized their own bridgeheads across the Rhine before Montgomery's spectacular crossing got underway, Bradley was highly delighted. 'To hell with the planners!' he cried when Hodges told him that the First had captured the Remagen bridge.

The situation was shaping up exactly in the way Bradley wanted it to. In spite of the difficulty of the terrain on the stretch of the Rhine proposed by Hodges as his starting point for his attack into the heart of the Reich (between Remagen and Koblenz), and the lack of good exit roads, Bradley knew by March 1945 that he was succeeding in drawing the Supreme Com-

mander away from his initial liking for the Montgomery plan. By 4th April, when his Ninth Army was returned to him from Montgomery, he knew he had won. The final single thrust into Germany was to be to the south, with Montgomery playing the role he, Bradley, had once played – that of the flank guard. The wheel had come the full circle.

It was useless to argue as Churchill did that the new strategy would have a decisive influence on the politics of post-war Europe. That eventuality interested neither Bradley nor the Supreme Commander nor even General Marshall back in Washington, who daily dealt with politicians of the highest rank. Montgomery could write later 'The Americans could not understand that it was of little avail to win the war strategically if we lost it politically; because of this curious viewpoint we suffered accordingly from VE-day onwards, and are still so suffering. War is a political instrument; once it is clear that you are going to win, political considerations must influence its further course. It became obvious to me in the autumn of 1944 that the way things were being handled was going to have repercussions far beyond the end of the war: it looked to me then as if we were going to "muck it up." I reckon we did.'

Thus, although, as I have written, we still do not have full details of Bradley's part in helping Eisenhower to make his fateful stop-on-the-Elbe decision, he must take a certain amount of responsibility for it. At first hesitantly and then deliberately he helped to force Eisenhower to realise the importance of his own southern command, in particular Patton's Third Army. As the breach between him and Montgomery became a matter of public knowledge after the Ardennes battle, Eisenhower realised that not only Bradley's reputation but his own might be involved if he allowed Montgomery his head in the north. Montgomery had to be stopped. But what could be offered militarily as a concession to American public in the last month of the war once the heart of Germany had been penetrated? Obviously not Berlin, but what about southern Germany? The result was that Bradley's southern axis of attack became the chief one.

So in the end Bradley won.

And, if we overlook the political implications of his victory, perhaps deservedly so, then in the final analysis General Bradley showed the most realistic approach to the campaign of all the senior commanders. For the battles the Allies were to fight in North West Europe after the D-Day landings were successfully accomplished were, in many ways, 'unlosable actions' once the lodging was accomplished, the Allies inherited a winning position against a beaten enemy. With their overwhelming strength and a beaten enemy, whose main effort was in the East anyway, the question was not whether the Germans could be beaten, but when and how.

Perhaps Montgomery's choice of place was right, but his choice of method was not. His approach (save for the completely untypical Arnhem plan) was slow and ponderous. Irrespective of the strength of the enemy confronting him or the terrain, he invariably built up enormous supplies of ammunition, arranged for immense bombing raids, and prepared gigantic numbers of vehicles prior to any operation. In many ways, his preparations were reminiscent of one of those First World War frontal attacks from which Montgomery had learned nothing in twenty-odd years save the need for overwhelming superiority of men and material and the use of machines to save men's lives.

Bradley, on the other hand, suspected the machines, sometimes to his cost as at 'Utah' beach. But unlike Montgomery he did not feel the need for such tremendous and often unnecessary preparations, which, for instance, in the case of Montgomery's Rhine crossing were like the labourings of elephant to produce a mouse. In the end his troops crossed the Rhine at the 'wrong' spot, the badly roaded and hilly stretch of the river between Remagen and Koblenz, and it made no real difference to speak of. His troops advanced out of the bridgehead as rapidly and as effectively as did Montgomery's debouching into the Ruhr and the Westphalian plains beyond.

Although he came from Missouri, Bradley still had about him something of the naive old-fashioned Yankee who suspected complicated set solutions. When we succeed in penetrating the armor he set up about himself, we see a man who was remarkably approachable by those below him, who was difficult to fool and not too often inclined to fool himself. Bradley tended to a more realistic approach

Bradley arrives in England for Atlantic Pact talks, 1949

Bradley represents the US on the Military Committee of NATO

than most of his fellows and he seized the opportunities and exploited them as they came. As a result he was more flexible than Montgomery and knew how to take advantage of any suitable opportunity when it came along. Montgomery did not. In the final analysis, one might say that while Bradley was an able tactician, he was not overly brilliant in the field of strategy. Montgomery, on the other hand, was an excellent, if limited, strategist. He tried to mould situations to his will, thinking strategically, while Bradley was often unable – or unwilling – to do so. He acted in answer to the dictates of the situation that is, he responded tactically. Chester Wilmot has summed up the difference between the two men as follows: 'He [Bradley] was successful in conducting operations so long as someone else was controlling the battle as a whole, preserving the balance of the force, manoeuvring the enemy into a vulnerable position and then developing the concentration necessary for a decisive stroke . . . The basic difference between Bradley and Montgomery was that, whereas Bradley moved at the dictates of the situation responding tactically, Montgomery endeavoured to mould situations to his will acting strategically'.

If this estimate of Bradley's ability is perhaps, to some extent, true, it is also true that the situation in NW Europe no longer needed the long-range strategic planning that Montgomery thought was necessary and that in the end the tactician was more effective and more relevant to the situation actually present on the battlefield than the strategist.

It is clear today twenty-five years after the end of the Second World War that most of the senior commanders involved in the last two years of the conflict on the Allied side were over-rated. Martin Blumenson, the US military historian, has called Montgomery 'vastly overrated, the most overrated general of World War II'. Naturally Mr Blumenson has a special axe to grind; he could well have applied his harsh judgement to most of Montgomery's fellow senior commanders. As Liddell Hart, the dean of military historians, has expressed it: 'Those who commanded in the field during the later phase of the war operated with an advantage of strength over the enemy too large to form an adequate test . . . Moreover, none of them in the main theatre proved their capacity to master adverse conditions and out-manoeuvre opponents of superior strength – which is the greatest test of generalship . . . The most successful of the Allied commanders enjoyed such an immense quantitative advantage that the qualitative value of their own performance cannot be gauged'.

Thus history will be kind to these commanders. After all they won. But with rare exceptions they were unable to prove themselves or their true qualities, for they were never faced with those adverse conditions which show a general for what he really is.

Even the surprise German counter-attack in the Ardennes does not allow us to see General Bradley under these circumstances, for in spite of the seriousness of the situation after 16th December 1944 – and the Ardennes counter attack was perhaps the most serious crisis facing the Western Allies during the whole 1944 – 1945 campaign – no one ever thought that it could lead to a defeat. That consideration never entered any of the leading commanders' heads (though General Patton once did tell his staff after a gruelling day in the last week of December during his advance against the southern flank of the German bulge, 'we can lose this war still'). At the most the German offensive could mean a set-back but never a defeat.

Thus we have no yardsticks to measure Omar Bradley as a great captain, like those great captains in the greatest war ever fought by the United States, that of 1861-1865. Unlike Grant or Lee, he was never forced to fight with his back to the wall against overwhelming odds or completely adverse circumstances. Throughout the North West European campaign, the big battalions were always on his side. There was never a chance that his actions, right or wrong, might contribute to his country losing the war.

But if Bradley cannot be regarded as a great captain, he will be remembered as a very able soldier, who grew appreciably in stature as the campaign went on and one who was a great advocate of the much maligned US Army; a jealous guardian of its honour and its prestige. If he was not 'the greatest battle line commander I have met in this war' (as General Eisenhower wrote in a personal letter to General Marshall in the last month of the campaign), he was very definitely a dedicated and highly professional *American* soldier, who did the best he could for his calling and his country, which I think, in the end effect, is all that such a modest person as Omar Nelson Bradley would profess to be . . .

Bibliography

The Struggle for Europe by Chester Wilmot (Collins, London. Harper & Row, New York)
A Soldier's Story by Omar Bradley (Eyre & Spottiswoode, London. Holt, Rhinehart & Winston, New York)
Patton: Ordeal and Triumph by L Farago (Arthur Baker, London. Astor-Honor, New York)
Crusade in Europe by Dwight Eisenhower (Doubleday, New York)
Intelligence at the Top by Sir K Strong (Cassell, London. Doubleday, New York)
My Three Years with Eisenhower by H Butcher (Heineman, New York)
Triumph and Tragedy by W Churchill (Cassell, London. Houghton & Mifflin, Boston)
War as I knew it by George Patton (Houghton & Mifflin)
The Second World War by J Fuller (Eyre & Spottiswoode, London)
Triumph in the West by Arthur Bryant (Collins, London. Doubleday, New York)